ORSAY

Paintings

Michel Laclotte
Former Curator of the Museums

Geneviève Lacambre
Curator of the Musée d'Orsay

Anne Distel
Chief Curator at the Musée d'Orsay

Claire Frèches-Thory
Chief Curator at the Musée d'Orsay

Marc Bascou
Chief Curator at the Musée d'Orsay

Foreword by Françoise Cachin
Director of the Musées de France

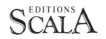

EDITIONS SCALA

Réunion des musées nationaux

© 1986, 1998, Éditions Scala

© SPADEM 1986 : Émile Bernard, Pierre Bonnard, Giovanni Boldini,
Maurice Denis, Aristide Maillol, Aman Jean, Ker-Xavier Roussel,
Édouard Vuillard, Maximilien Luce

© ADAGP 1986 : Pierre Bonnard, Albert Marquet, Alfons Mucha,
James Ensor

Design : Maxence Scherf
Cover design : Philippe Hubert
Translation : Anthony Roberts
Photos : Réunion des musées nationaux - Paris

Preface

Since this book was first published, on the occasion of the Musée d'Orsay's opening in December 1986, several million visitors have seen the pictures reproduced here in their new surroundings. Some came from prestigious collections such as the Jeu de Paume or the Louvre, whilst others were unearthed from the storehouses or vaults to which they had been relegated for half a century by the prevailing fashion, which has been swifter to admire works heralding the 20th century than to look, without preconceptions, at past achievements.

Michel Laclotte, who since 1986 has directed the museum's conceptual team, describes the history of these collections in greater detail. By opening the museum, we wanted to display the best of what had been hidden by a triumphant modernity, without calling excellence into question. The museum's painting collections have, therefore, continued to enrich this perspective.

We have superb donations to thank for works of outstanding importance such as the *Étude pour les Joueurs de cartes* by Cézanne or *La Nuit étoilée* by Van Gogh. Other masterpieces by Daubigny, Courbet (*L'Origine du Monde*), Monet (the central part of his big *Déjeuner sur l'herbe*), Renoir, Degas, Cézanne, Signac, Bonnard, Vuillard and a magnificent set of fifteen decorative panels by Odilon Redon have fortunately been assigned to the Musée d'Orsay after being accepted by the State under the dation system, in lieu of capital transfer or inheritance tax.

Bold purchases have also enabled us to buy in missing paintings by Gérôme or Renoir in New York, and safeguard the retention in France of notable works by Gustave Moreau (*Galatée*), Gauguin (*Autoportrait au Christ jaune*) or Bonnard (*Le Voyage*).

The continual efforts being made at the same time to fill gaps in the field of foreign painting must also be emphasised. Works as diverse as *Variations in purple and green* by the American painter Whistler, a subtle, Japanese influenced view of the Thames, *Siesta* by the German artist Hans Thoma, a rustic idyll in the tradition of classical landscapes, the disturbing painting *Moonlight* by the Dutch artist Breitner, a rare Pointillist seascape by the Belgian painter Lemmen, and Mondrian's still figurative *Departure of the fishing boats* take their place in a wider vista of western painting, particularly at the point when the nineteenth century makes way for the twentieth. Among our most recent acquisitions *Hvile* (*Repose*) by the Danish painter Hammershøi, a timeless, silent reverie, provides a striking contrast with the vibrant *View of Capolago* by the Swiss artist Giovanni Giacometti, whose chromatic approach can be compared with contemporaneous landscapes by Hodler and Munch.

Only the most important new acquisitions now on display have been mentioned here, but we hope that this book will encourage the reader to return soon to the Musée d'Orsay : in the years ahead many new discoveries will await and welcome you.

Introduction

The Musée d'Orsay offers a panorama of late 19th- and early 20th-century art. In addition its programme of temporary exhibitions, concerts and audio-visual events lends itself to all forms of interdisciplinary encounters, stressing the complexity of an epoch which was incomparably rich in artistic experience and variety. To avoid confusion and surfeit, the planning of the museum's permanent exhibition rooms is clearly based on distinctions between techniques and modes of expression; hence, it is easy enough to plan and describe a general tour of the museum, linking the various display rooms while identifying each in a separate way. The aim of this book is to define such a tour, and at the same time to offer a history of painting from about 1850 to the early years of our own century, as illustrated by the collections of the Musée d'Orsay.

Before we go into the history of these collections, we should perhaps explain the timespan covered by the museum's programmes. This timespan is circumscribed by the Louvre on one side and the Musée national d'Art moderne on the other.

The latter borderline is one that obtrudes quite naturally, i.e. the Musée d'Orsay ends where the Musée d'Art moderne begins, in the tumultuous years of 1904-1907 which saw the birth of a completely new pictorial language in fauvism and expressionism, schools which were themselves nurtured by the post-impressionist experience prior to the stunning challenge of the *Demoiselles d'Avignon* (1907). One might add that these years also saw radical changes in architecture and design, with the decline of Art Nouveau as a standard; for example, the Wienerwerkstätte were created post 1903.

It was less easy, however, to determine a preliminary date for a cut-off within the monolithic 19th century. 1863, the year of the Salon des Refusés, has sometimes been quoted as a suitable juncture; but in fact 1863 was only really important in terms of French painting, and represents no break in continuity where the other arts are concerned. A further step backward to include the romantic period, which was another possibility, would have required more hanging space than the Musée d'Orsay could supply (in particular for huge canvases like those of Géricault, Delacroix and the Louis-Philippe painters). Thus the decision was taken to set the museum's early limit at 1848-1850, a time which was redolent of change in every sphere and not only in the political, economic and social ones.

This time-frame contains the public recognition of Millet and Courbet, and with them of "realism", at the Salons of 1849 and 1850-1855; the foundation of the Pre-Raphaelite Brotherhood in 1848; and the construction of the Crystal Palace (1850-51) and the Nouveau Louvre (from 1852 onwards). The essential role of the first universal exhibitions (London, 1851, Paris, 1855) in the development of historic eclecticism and the confrontation between art and industry was yet another aspect that marked a fundamental mid-century renewal in every area of artistic creativity.

In order to mitigate the arbitrary effect of this cut-off date, a certain amount of transitional leeway has been allowed. The first exhibition rooms contain a few later works by great artists of 1800-1850 who continued to be active and influential in succeeding years. These include Ingres and his school, Delacroix, Chassériau, Corot, Rousseau and the Barbizon landscape painters, the bulk of whose production nonetheless remains in the Louvre. Likewise, the end of the period makes a brief allusion to fauvism, the development of which is taken up fully in the first "chapter" of the Musée d'Art moderne.

The principal source of the collections which are today assembled at the Musée d'Orsay was the Musée du Luxembourg, founded in 1818 by Louis XVIII to house "the paintings and sculptures of the modern school". Until the creation of the Musée national d'Art moderne in 1937, the Musée du Luxembourg contained a selection of state-owned works of art by living artists. The rule was that after the death of an artist "whose merit was endorsed by universal acclaim", his work would receive the supreme honour of entering the Louvre, after a period of purgatory which varied according to the times.

Hence the Musée du Luxembourg for years represented official taste, its only sources being the Salons; and the Salons in turn were the only vehicles by which an artist could make his work known to the public, on condition that he were admitted to them. In reaction to a period of openness to living art (Delacroix and Ingres were exhibited side by side from 1824 onwards), the criteria of selection narrowed considerably in the mid-19th century. After a liberal hiatus in 1848-1851, when Corot, Théodore Rousseau, Rosa Bonheur and Antigna were finally admitted (while Courbet's *Après-dîner à Ornans* was acquired for the Musée de Lille), the Musée du Luxembourg reverted to a more limited view of contemporary art. This was personified by the more innocuous landscape artists, and history and genre painters of reliable eclectic quality. Excluded, of course, were the strongest representatives of realism : the absence, in their lifetimes, of Courbet and Millet demonstrated a narrowness of outlook which naturally devolved on to the younger school headed by Manet.

Despite the efforts of its remarkable curator, Philippe de Chennevières, who became director of the Beaux-Arts in 1873 (after trying in vain to acquire Courbet's masterpiece, *Le Combat de cerfs* in 1861), the Luxembourg remained firmly opposed to new ideas throughout the 1870s and 1880s, although the purchase of works by Millet (1875), Diaz (1877), Daubigny (1878) finally introduced some of the great older painters who had been neglected or bypassed.

The posthumous rehabilitation of Corot, Courbet, Millet and the Barbizon painters was carried out at the Louvre, its first manifestation being the acquisition of a number of Courbets at auction, and the gift of his *Enterrement à Ornans* by his sister. After this, the museum was presented with private donations of very fine works (Millet's *Printemps*, given by Mme Hartmann in 1887, and *Les Glaneuses*, given by Mme Pommery in 1880 when the artist's popularity was at its height), along with several complete collections.

The Louvre was also enriched by the collection of Thomy Thiéry, an art lover from Mauritius who had taken up residence in France. This copious and immaculately chosen group of paintings includes works by the Barbizon masters, as well as Corot and Delacroix. Rather than break up the unity of the ensemble, it was decided that the Thiéry collection should be kept intact at the Louvre and not moved to the Musée d'Orsay; in any case, most of the artists represented belong to the Louvre's allotted timespan. The presence of a few artists who properly belong in the Musée d'Orsay (such as Millet and Daubigny) will enable visitors to the Louvre to establish the necessary links between the 1830 school, the Barbizon school and their realist successors.

In order to achieve the reverse manœuvre, ie. to provide an adequate representation of the Barbizon painters at the Musée d'Orsay, a similar collection is exhibited there, that of Alfred Chauchard, one of the founders of the Magasins du Louvre department store. The costly Chauchard collection, which came to the Louvre in 1909, is typical of the taste of many wealthy French and Americans of the time (apart from Thomy Thiéry, we may cite the collectors of Rheims, who left a magnificent legacy to their city). To Alfred Chauchard belongs the distinction of bringing Millet's *Angélus* home from America, at the then exorbitant price of 800·000 francs. His collection at the Musée d'Orsay offers a magnificent ensemble of works by Millet, the Barbizon school, Corot, Delacroix, Decamps and Meissonier.

Chennevières had dreamed of giving wall space to Manet and his pupils, as he did for Puvis de Chavannes. Of course, this project was never realised, and Manet did not receive the blessing of the Luxembourg in his lifetime, any more than Courbet or Millet. All the same, the first battle to open the Museum to the impressionists was waged in his name. In 1890 *Olympia* was purchased from Mme Manet, who was preparing to sell it to an American collector, by a group of subscribers organised by Monet. The painting was subsequently donated to the state and the Musée du Luxembourg. The following year, another classic masterpiece of modern art, Whistler's *Mother*, was bought by a similar group which included Mallarmé and Clemenceau. By contrast, the first Renoir to enter the Museum, *Jeunes filles au piano*, was a recent work, practically done to order. This painting arrived in the same year, 1892, that the images of Monet, Bazille and Renoir himself appeared at the Luxembourg, grouped around Manet in Fantin-Latour's *Atelier des Batignolles*.

With the 1896 bequest of the painter Caillebotte, their friend and patron, the impressionists finally reached the Luxembourg in force : seven Degas pastels, two Manets (one being *Le Balcon*), two Cézannes, eight Monets, six Renoirs (including *Le Moulin de la Galette*), six Sisleys and seven Pissarros.

But this invasion was not accomplished without difficulty and only a part of Caillebotte's collection was ultimately accepted. The "affaire Caillebotte" caused, and still causes, considerable controversy. It has been recognised as convincing proof of the blindness of officialdom to living art. Even though this judgement may be tempered to some extent and certain functionaries can be excused (the national committee of museum curators did, after all, accept the entire bequest), the fact remains that those responsible for the national collection rejected no less than twenty-nine paintings by Cézanne, Manet, Renoir, Sisley and Pissarro, and subsequently continued to reject them despite the entreaties of Martial Caillebotte. In 1897, the opening of a room devoted to impressionist works from the Caillebotte bequest, in an annex of the Orangerie (opened as part of the Luxembourg in 1886), prompted an official protest from the Académie des Beaux-Arts. The Académie was incensed that paintings that were "flawed to the point of extravagance" could be hung alongside "the finest examples of contemporary French art".

Throughout the final third of the 19th century, the Musée du Luxembourg collection was regularly and abundantly expanded by purchases at the Salons and by gifts. The painters selected were not all conservative, as is proved by the acquisition of works by Fantin-Latour, Puvis de Chavannes, Carrière and later by the younger artists of the Bande Noire, to cite only a few examples. Nonetheless, the museum is dominated by ancient and modern historical paintings with exemplary subject matter, fashions and society portraiture, and naturalist paintings. Naturalist art, with sources of inspiration ranging from the populist to the symbolic, evolved clear and often brilliant modernist techniques of its own, eventually accounting for the bulk of late 19th-century output outside avant-garde circles.

At this point, thanks to the labours of its curator, Léonce Bénédite, the museum was finally opened to non-French schools of painting, with many foreign artists following Whistler's pioneering example. Doubtless it will be regretted that such painters as Munch, Ensor, Hodler, Klimt and Segantini were overlooked, but at the same time rare works such as Winslow Homer's *Summer Night* (1900) and a remarkable series of Italian canvases by Pelizza da Volpedo (1910) were found and acquired. After a gift of several British paintings by Edmund Davis (1915), the foreign section of the Luxembourg had enough individual works (420) to warrant the opening of a separate museum at the Jeu de Paume in 1922.

Meanwhile, two generous collectors had endowed the Louvre, and the French national heritage, with impressionist paintings of the very highest quality. The first of these benefactors was Etienne Moreau-Nélaton (1859-1927), whose work on Corot, Delacroix, Millet and Manet places him among the finest art historians of his time. His donation of paintings, complemented at his death by a large series of drawings by Corot, Delacroix and Millet, make up a unique ensemble of the 1830 school (this part of the collection has remained at the Louvre). In addition, there was Fantin-Latour's *Hommage à Delacroix*, and major works by Monet, Sisley, Pissarro and Manet, dominated by the *Déjeuner sur l'herbe*. The collection was presented to the Musée des Arts décoratifs in 1906, and moved to the Louvre in 1934.

The collection of comte Isaac de Camando (1851-1911), a banker and amateur of 18th-century French art, was bequeathed to the nation in 1911. It admirably completes and balances the Caillebotte and Moreau-Nélaton collections with a sumptuous series of Degas, some late Monets, five Cézannes, and the first Lautrecs and Van Goghs acquired by the museum, in addition to works by the masters mentioned earlier.

Thenceforward, the impressionists were officially accepted. The Luxembourg collection continued to grow, chiefly by dint of private generosity. This took the form of gifts by artists' heirs (Caillebotte, 1894 ; Toulouse-Lautrec, 1902 ; Renoir, 1923 ; Bazille, 1924 ; Monet, 1930 ; Pissarro, 1930) ; gifts from models (Degas' Dihaus and Manet's Zolas) ; and, above all, gifts from collectors. In 1929, the transfer of the impressionists to the Louvre marked the triumph of a school of painting whose fame gradually eclipsed that of all the other late 19th century movements. When their time came, many former stars of the old Luxembourg found themselves refused admission to the Louvre, and they were subsequently dispersed around France.

The lack of means available to national museums between the two wars was all the more regrettable because the talents of the great art dealers and the demand created by collectors had by then flooded the French market with canvases by the innovators of the second half of the 19th century. These innovators were by now regarded as great masters, and included names like Courbet, Corot or Daumier alongside the impressionists. Inevitably, many paintings went abroad, although some were retained at the 1918 Degas sale (*Sémiramis, La Famille Belleli*) as well as Monet's *Les Femmes au jardin* (1921), and Gauguin's *Le Cheval blanc* (1927). Courbet's *Atelier* was acquired in

1920 by public subscription, supported by the Amis du Louvre. Nonetheless, apart from these brilliant exceptions, the French national heritage suffered an irremediable loss with the departure of many paintings by Cézanne, Gauguin and Seurat, which French museums either could not, or would not, prevent.

In 1937, the Musée du Luxembourg was abolished and replaced by the Musée national d'Art moderne at the Palais de Tokyo, which had been built for the Universal Exhibition. The Musée d'Art moderne reopened after the war with its collections greatly enriched by Jean Cassou's aggressive policy of acquisition (purchases and gifts by artists). At that time it offered a panorama of modern art beginning in 1890, ie. neo-impressionism (without Seurat), the Pont-Aven school (without Gauguin) and the nabis ; certain aspects of "fin de siècle" art, such as produced by the painters of "la vie parisienne", were also peripherally represented.

The reorganisation of the Louvre, which had begun before the war and continued after 1946, produced one spectacular innovation. The Jeu de Paume took up the Louvre's impressionist collections, from Boudin, Jongkind and Guigou to Seurat, Lautrec and the Douanier Rousseau. After the dark war years, the opening of the impressionist museum in 1947 in the glorious light of the Tuileries had a symbolic effect at a time when younger artists were yearning for pure painting.

The ensemble of collections on exhibition is impressive, with a number of undispersed groupings that illustrate the taste of certain great benefactors (the collection of Antonin Personnaz, rich in Monets, Pissarros and Lautrecs, which was given in 1937). Its abundance, we repeat, is wholly due to the unselfishness and sense of civic obligation of art patrons, too numerous to name ; but we should at least mention the magnificent gesture of Mme de Goldschmidt-Rothschild, who sent a telegram to the Directeur des musées de France on the day of the liberation of Paris, to announce her intention of leaving her most precious possession, Van Gogh's *Arlésienne*, to the Louvre.

Fortunately, an increased budget support from the Amis du Louvre and revenue from an anonymous Canadian donor (linked to the memory of the princesse de Polignac, who in 1943 bequeathed her paintings by Monet and Manet) allowed the museum to make certain vital purchases in the following years (notably works by Seurat, Cézanne and Redon). Other art lovers, meanwhile, gave their finest pieces (J. Laroche, 1947 ; Dr and Mme A. Charpentier, 1951 ; M. and Mme Frédéric Lung, 1961 ; baronne Gourgaud, 1965). The peace treaty with Japan brought some remarkable pieces from the Matsukata collection (1959). Finally, three entire new collections came to the Jeu de Paume : the collection of Dr Gachet, with eight Van Goghs (1949-1954) ; Eduardo Mollard (1961) ; and the collection of Max and Rosy Kaganovitch (1973), extending from Daumier to Derain.

As a result of this torrent of new paintings, the Jeu de Paume premises became too small for the large crowds of visitors which came flocking to see them and could no longer provide conditions of comfort and security. Thus when the old Gare d'Orsay was classified a historic building and its demolition averted, the decision was made in 1977 to install a new museum there, covering the art of the second half of the 19th century and the beginning of the 20th, ie. impressionism and post-impressionism. At a stroke, this solved the problem created by the Musée d'Art moderne's move to the Centre Pompidou in 1976, which had resulted in the rejection of a number of works considered too old to merit a place in its programme. These included the paintings of the Pont-Aven school, the neo-impressionists, the nabi group and a mass of "fin de siècle" French and foreign artists who had been kept in reserve for many years and whom both the history of art and contemporary fashions were now bringing back into favour. Hence the Musée d'Orsay is composed of the Jeu de Paume collections, the collections left at the Palais de Tokyo by the Musée d'Art moderne (exhibited between 1977 and 1986 as a prefiguration of the Musée d'Orsay, under the banner of post-impressionism); and, lastly, paintings from the Louvre from the second half of the 19th century which were not displayed at the Jeu de Paume.

Yet, even assembled under one roof, it was doubted that the new Orsay collections would suffice to give a true idea of this extraordinarily fertile era. We know only too well how much our views of 19th-century art have altered in the last twenty-five years. For example, a series of rediscoveries and reassessments at the "Sources du vingtième siècle" (a memorable exhibition organised in Paris in 1961) brought to light the modernistic trends linked to symbolism and Art Nouveau. Also revealed were the merits of certain artists hitherto unjustly condemned as frumpish and conventional, along with a number of other European and American painters who had long been overshadowed and excluded by the French school.

In consequence, a vigorous acquisition policy was initiated in 1978 with a view to balancing Orsay's motley collections, strengthening some sections, and filling gaps in others wherever possible.

Since that date, about 1000 new paintings have entered the museum. In the first instance, these were works that already belonged to the national collections and which were recovered from the various public premises (museums and administrative buildings) where they had come to rest, either because of the somewhat incoherent dispersion of the Luxembourg collection between the wars, or through the direct attribution of the Service des œuvres d'art de l'État.

This tactic produced a harvest of about thirty paintings, which were of course replaced by other works of art, according to the wishes of the curators concerned. These paintings mainly served to reinforce the selection of realists between 1848-1860 (Breton, Antigna, Pils, Jacque, Troyon, Vollon, etc.), certain aspects of Second Empire "eclecticism" (Tissot, Legros, Cabanel, etc.), and the official art of the Third Republic (Lhermitte, Gervex, de Neuville, Weerts, Henri Martin). The national museums (Compiègne, Fontainebleau) also contributed, with Versailles generously offering a valuable series of portraits (Hippolyte Flandrin, Baudry, Bonnat, Sargent, Meissonier, Forain). To the Musée des Arts décoratifs we owe Maurice Denis' painted decoration for the chapelle du Vésinet. Two other decorative ensembles were saved from an uncertain fate and restored : one by Luc-Olivier Merson for the stairway of a private townhouse (1901) and the other a grandiose mythological sequence painted by René Ménard for the Paris Law Faculty.

The second source of the museum's enrichment has been the generosity of private citizens, in some cases supported by the recently established Société des Amis du musée d'Orsay, or by the Lutèce Foundation. Among the many gifts received by the museum, we would mention a few presented by heirs of artists, which have resulted in a better representation of the work of Sérusier (the Boutaric legacy), Mucha (the gift of Jiri Mucha, 1979), Cappiello (the gift of Mme Cappiello, 1981) and above all Odilon Redon, ostracised for so long by French museums (the gift of Ari and Suzanne Redon, 1984, of 542 individual works, including 91 paintings and pastels).

Thanks to regular purchases since 1904 (Vuillard, *Le Déjeuner du matin*) and donations (Vuillard, 1941, with many works by the artist ; Reine Natanson ; Bernheim de Villers, with family portraits by Bonnard, Vuillard and Renoir, etc.) the nabis were already very well represented in the original stocks of the Musée d'Art moderne. Bonnard's nabi period is incomparably demonstrated at the museum, as a result of an opportune series of donations (notably *La Partie de croquet*, given by M. Daniel Wildenstein through the Société des Amis du musée d'Orsay ; the *Garden*, given by M. Jean-Claude Bellier ; the *Portrait de Claude Terrasse*, given by his son Charles) and « dation » (donation in lieu of inheritance tax) (*Femme au jardin*).

The museum has benefitted from a particularly glittering series of donations in lieu of inheritance tax, which have enriched its entire repertoire. These range from Courbet (*La Truite*, *La Femme au chien*) to Matisse (*Luxe, calme et volupté*), Manet (*Combat de taureaux*, *Évasion de Rochefort*), Monet (*La Rue Montorgueil*, *Jardin à Giverny*), Pissarro, Renoir (*La Danse à la ville*, paired with *La Danse à la campagne*, purchased in 1979), Redon (*Eve*, and two pastels, *Vitrail* and *le Char d'Appollon*). In 1982, the series of five Cézannes which were originally in the collection of Auguste Pellerin rejoined those with which the generosity of this great art lover and his children had already endowed the museum : three still lifes (1929), *La Femme à la cafetière* (1956), and *Emperaire* (1964). Though it naturally does not fail to include great works which would otherwise have left France (like Monet's *La Pie*), the Musée d'Orsay's purchasing programme until its opening was intended to give priority to artists who were ill-represented, or represented not at all, in the collections. Hence a particular though still insufficient effort has been made in regard to foreign schools (Klimt, Munch, Böcklin, Burne-Jones, Khnopff, Strindberg, Stück, Breitner, etc.).

As far as France is concerned, the museum is above all trying to strengthen its inventory of older masters from the Louvre (Ingres, *Venus* ; Delacroix, *Chasse aux lions* ; Huet ; Isabey, *Saint Antoine*, given by the Amis du musée d'Orsay). In addition, it is seeking to develop certain areas that have been neglected since the war, notably neo-impressionism and the school of Pont-Aven. A stimulus had already been given to the first of these schools by the generosity of Ginette Signac (Signac, Cross, Théo van Rysselberghe) ; this was followed by the purchase of works by Signac, Luce, Théo van Rysselberghe and Lemmen. As to Pont-Aven, after the 1977 purchase of Bernard's *Madeleine au bois d'Amour*, other works by Bernard and Serusier have come to the museum, notably *Le Talisman*.

Now that the Musée d'Orsay is finally opening its doors, can it be said that the history it relates is complete and objective ? Certainly not. A museum is not, and can never be, a coldly constructed encyclopaedia, signed, sealed and delivered. It is bound to reflect the tastes and preferences of the people responsible for its gradual construction over the years. Many masters are still lacking, and many schools and movements in art—especially foreign ones—are scarcely even mentioned. Let us hope that the future will be rich in surprises and changes ; and that by alterations, additions and subtractions we shall continue to perfect the reflection we offer today of an epoch in ferment, full of stimulating and fascinating contradictions.

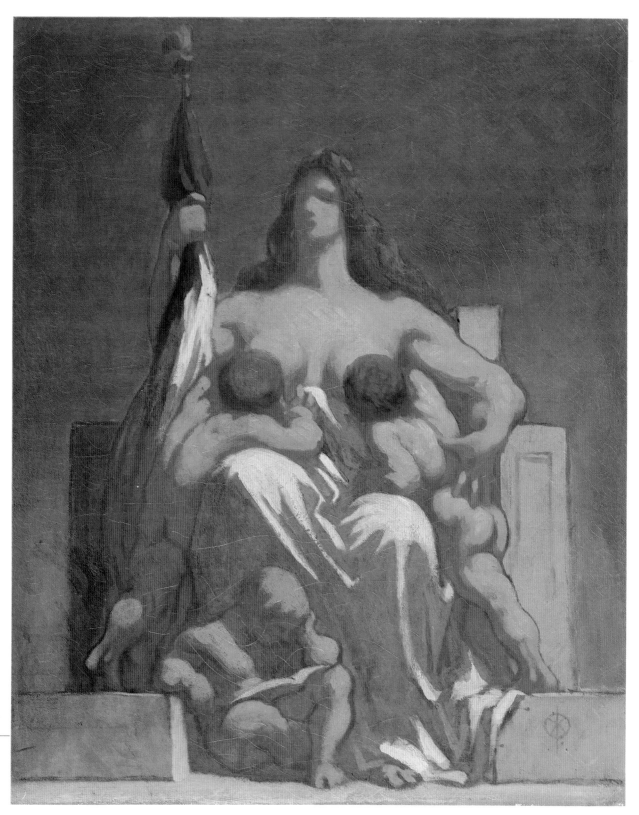

Honoré Daumier (1808-1879)
La République
Sketch submitted for the competition opened in 1848
by the directorate of the Beaux-Arts
73 × 60
Donated by Etienne Moreau-Nélaton, 1906

Eclectism and realism

The days of February 1848, which brought down the July Monarchy, were of the highest political importance in that they ignited other revolutions all across Europe. 1848 also had immediate repercussions for artists, whose lives had previously been dominated by the Salon : because it was up to the jury of the Salon, which was composed of members of the Académie des Beaux-Arts, to make its choice among the works presented. The artists they favoured found themselves able not only to reach potential private buyers, but also to sell to the most prestigious public institution as far as art was concerned, the Musée du Luxembourg, which collected the best works of living artists. One of the first acts of the 1848 republican administration was to open a Salon at the Louvre without a jury ; the experiment was not repeated, since the Salon attracted too many inexperienced amateurs, but it did allow a few ostracized artists like Courbet to become known. 1848 was also the year that the government organized a public competition for a figure symbolizing the Republic ; this produced all kinds of paintings in the usual allegorical tradition, but among the twenty painted sketches which were selected for full-size execution was one by Daumier, then at the start of his career. As an enthusiastic republican, Daumier had produced a powerful rendering of the motto ''The Republic feeds and educates its children''. He was never to complete the larger version, but he kept the sketch, which finally entered the Louvre in 1906 as part of the Moreau-Nélaton donation. After 1848 there followed several years of support for a type of painting which had formerly been condemned, along with a reassessment of the hierarchical academy of genres. But despite a gradual reversion to traditional structures, particularly as far as the jury of the Salon was concerned, a real break did take place in many areas which subsequently affected the art of the Second Empire.

The first fruits of this had already begun to appear before 1848 ; for the painting of historical themes, apart from the development of a neo-Grecian trend and the debut of Jean-Léon Gérôme, the 1847 Salon was distinguished by the much-remarked late arrival of a huge composition by Thomas Couture (1815-1879), *Les Romains de la décadence* ; this had been ordered by the administration in 1846, and was later exhibited in the Musée du Luxembourg in 1851. In the orgiastic theme of the painting and the attitudes of the figures (which were considered trivial at the time) we may detect the first stirrings of realism : nonetheless, the myriad references to the art of the past, including Veronese, Tiepolo and Poussin, make this a fine example of eclecticism, with its clear colours and broadly brushed, almost chalky architecture.

In 1853, during the first Salon of the Second Empire, the evolution of history painting towards the format of the genre scene became noticeable with the ''demi-nature'' figures in two paintings acquired for the Musée du Luxembourg, Chassériau's *Tepidarium* and Benouville's *Saint François*.

These works were exhibited again in the Palais des Beaux-Arts, a temporary edifice built for the 1855 Universal Exhibition which Napoleon III organised along the same lines as the 1851 exhibition at the Crystal Palace,

London, an event which had brought much credit to Queen Victoria and Prince Albert. By comparison with London, it was an innovation to ask living artists from all nations to take part in a retrospective exhibition; the result was a fabulous temporary museum filled with the art of the preceding decades. All the major paintings of Ingres and Delacroix, the two personalities who dominated the contemporary art scene, were displayed; and today, while most of their work remains in the Louvre, the Musée d'Orsay nonetheless possesses a few later pieces. Ingres, who had for years boycotted the Salon, sent some recent paintings to the Universal Exhibition, notably his *Vierge à l'hostie*, ordered by the State and completed in 1854. He completed *La Source* in 1856, the ownership of which was hotly contended for by rich collectors after a private viewing in his studio. The battle was eventually won by comte Duchâtel, and in 1878 his widow bequeathed this painting, hailed at the time by Théophile Gautier as a masterpiece, a ''pure Parian marble with the bloom of life'', to the museums of France. Against Ingres, the undisputed master of line, stood Delacroix, the romantic colourist. His *Chasse aux lions* sketch, ordered in 1854 for the Bordeaux Museum and first exhibited in 1855, has now been acquired by the Musée d'Orsay. This impetuously painted work with its pure colours remained in the artist's studio until his death, after which it was shown in a number of exhibitions and influenced many young painters, notably Manet, Renoir, Signac and Matisse.

The Musée du Luxembourg would always admit works by painters who completed their studies at the Beaux-Arts, won the Prix de Rome, and then returned from Italy to enter the Académie des Beaux-Arts and receive their nomination as teachers at the Ecole. Thus Cabanel won the Prix de Rome in 1845, Baudry and Bouguereau in 1850, Delaunay in 1856 and Regnault in 1866. Regnault was Cabanel's pupil, and Cabanel, like Bouguereau, had been the pupil of Picot : so, an academic tradition was perpetuated, one which had begun with neo-classicism but which gradually lost its heroic subject matter and replaced it with pure fantasy. Although mythological themes persisted in the work of painters like Bouguereau (1825-1905) until the end of the century, they were rapidly supplanted by Early Christian motifs—Delaunay's *Peste à Rome* is a good example—or subjects drawn from the history of the Middle Ages. The Orient was another theme—see the Moorish kings depicted by Regnault, a bright young hope who was killed in action in 1871—along with French history, as drawn by Jean-Paul Laurens (1838-1921), who later became the official image maker of the Third Republic. At the end of 1912, Lauren's work joined that of Jules Lefèbvre, Aimé Morot and Raphaël Collin in an exhibition at the Galerie Georges Petit, revelling in the title of ''Pompiers'' (conventional artists). Apollinaire noted at the time that ''academic art is out of fashion...'', though perhaps he had his own reasons for saying so. The meticulous representation of military life by Meissonier shows a slightly different tendency, which derived from the study of the Flemish and Dutch painters at the Louvre. The artist, who was made a member of the Institut in 1861, had an extraordinary success with collectors, selling his smaller works for enormous sums of money. Meissonier eventually became the first president of the Société nationale des Beaux-Arts; in 1890, the Société founded a new Salon in opposition to that of the over-traditional Artistes français, which in 1881 had replaced the official Salon.

In 1891, Meissonier was succeeded as president of the new Salon by a fellow artist from Lyons who had moved to Paris, Puvis de Chavannes (1824-1898). Puvis had been famous ever since the Second Empire for his decorative paintings installed in various public buildings, such as the Amiens Museum and the Panthéon in Paris. However, he was not represented at the Musée du Luxembourg until the 1887 purchase of his *Pauvre pêcheur*. It is typical that his huge, light-filled composition *L'Été*, from the 1873 Salon, was destined for a provincial museum ; it was only recently assigned to the Musées nationaux and the Musée d'Orsay. Indeed, the Luxembourg often held only one example of an artist's work : this was the case of Gustave Moreau's celebrated *Orphée* in the 1866 Salon. Only after Moreau's death in 1898 did some of his admirers—led by Charles Hayem—make a gift to the museum of other important paintings and aquarelles, whilst the painter himself bequeathed to the State a museum he had built to house the thousands of studies and frequently unfinished paintings he had amassed in fifty years of work.

To perfect his training, Moreau had travelled to Italy, like his friend Puvis de Chavannes, or Degas, whom he met there. Degas, at an early stage in his career, was tempted by historical painting, as is clear in his *Séminaris construisant Babylone*. It is significant that this painting was one of the first of Degas' works acquired by the Musée du Luxembourg just after his death in 1918. While older painters like Corot made several trips to Italy, prior to scouring the length and breadth of France in search of subject matter, others systematically abandoned this tradition in favour of a close study of the French countryside and the life of their native provinces.

In the end, this guarantee of great art, identified by the academic guardians of eclecticism in constant references to the past, ceased to satisfy a certain breed of artists which preferred sincerity and direct observation of nature. Under Louis-Philippe, these artists were frequently barred from the Salon, but their moment of glory came under the short-lived Second Republic, when they gleaned such honours that they were subsequently exempted from submitting their works to the judgement of the jury, or even from exhibiting them—though for all that they still sold nothing to the Luxembourg.

This was the case of Millet and Courbet, some of whose paintings were timidly introduced to the Luxembourg soon after their deaths. 1875 witnessed the appearance of Millet's sober *Église de Greville* ; and in 1878 *La Vague* by Courbet was exhibited, followed in 1881 by his two self-portraits, which had been purchased at auction after his death. The problem with both Millet and Courbet was that the administration was shocked by their techniques and outraged by their choice of subjects.

While Daumier's astonishingly vigorous and modern paintings went almost unnoticed until the 1878 exhibition at the Galerie Durand-Ruel, those of the Barbizon painters (Théodore Rousseau, Diaz or Dupré), who had in some instances become famous prior to 1848, were aimed at a private clientèle. A market for the Barbizon painters quickly developed, and became progressively better organised on an international scale. The idea was that the museum should offer serious art, fit to set an example to artists and bolster France's predominant position in the field. This could exclude from the Luxembourg the works of painters who might simultaneously be on the Emperor's Civil List (along with Cabanel, Courbet or Corot) or in the directorate of the Beaux-Arts for the provinces, or even in the Civil Service. Daubigny is an interesting case in point : for years he was represented at the Luxembourg by a stolid landscape of Optevoz (subsequently moved to Rouen). Yet his *Moisson* exhibited at the 1852 Salon, with its stunning horizon in pure, simply-juxtaposed colours of red and yellow, was originally purchased for the premises of the Justice Ministry and only reached the Louvre in 1907.

Daubigny, like the Barbizon painters, was not afraid to take his easel out of doors and away from the cold north light of the studio. In his boat the *Botin*, he toured the rivers of the Ile de France and observed the reflections of light on water, as Monet later did. It is known, too, that Daubigny supported Manet's group of young naturalist painters as much as possible after he was elected to the jury of the Salon in 1864.

Millet was also interested in landscapes, particularly after 1863. Since 1848, while adhering to the small genre format, he had contrived to elevate the representation of labour in the fields to the same status as that of historical themes. Thus he created a whole series of works in the vein of *Les Glaneuses* or *L'Angelus* which attained great celebrity after 1880 but which horrified conservative critics and inspectors from the Beaux-Arts under the Second Empire. All the same, Millet had no lack of admirers, especially post 1860; for example, Frédéric Hartman ordered from him a series of four seasons which was never completed—though we do possess *Le Printemps*, a painting of luminous, dewy freshness which delicately and symbolically blends the presence of man with the awakening of nature. Again, Emile Gavet encouraged Millet to use pastel techniques, as in the stunning *Bouquet de marguerites* where he returns to the lightness of touch shown in his early work but this time in the context of naturalism. This pastel, which was purchased at the 1875 Gavet sale by Henri Rouart, was an influence in the development of Degas, who was, as we know, a friend of the Rouart family.

The lack of connection between the attitudes of the public and the artistic community, on the one hand, and that of the administration, with its high sense of its own mission, on the other, is highlighted by the misfortunes that befell the first of Corot's paintings, and the only one in his lifetime to enter the Luxembourg (in 1854, *Une matinée—La Danse des nymphes*). For the 1850-1851 Salon, Corot had taken the precaution of including a few nymphs in his *Matin*, a misty evocation of a site on the Palatine Hill at Rome which he had seen as a young man. That year, Corot himself was appointed to the jury; nonetheless, the staff of the Salon placed his painting in reserve, as though it had been damaged. Following a protest by one of the painter's friends, the painting was retrieved and acquired as a gesture of courtesy by the directorate of the Beaux-Arts, which was subsequently in no hurry to find a home for it. Finally, on the insistence of Philippe de Chennevières, it was admitted to the Luxembourg when Corot was fifty-eight.

Although Corot courted scandal vigorously in the first years of the Second Empire (in 1855 he responded to a partial rebuff from the jury of the Universal Exhibition by opening a private pavilion at the Alma under the banner of realism), nonetheless his most cherished desire was for recognition. Like other artists of the time, such as Jules Breton or Alexandre Antigna, he undertook large paintings with lifesize figures to depict contemporary everyday subjects; but his goal in doing so was to gain for his sincere and modern view of art the pre-eminent respect hitherto accorded to historical painting. The logical consequence was that *Un enterrement à Ornans*, *L'Atelier*, and *Le Combat de cerfs*, his largest paintings, found no buyers in his lifetime. Nor did *Le Départ des pompiers courant à un incendie*, which is now at the Petit Palais.

Courbet, who was accused of "painting ugliness" could be charming with boudoir scenes (*La Femme au chien*) or accessible, with his pictures of the Franche-Comté woodlands teeming with deer. These themes were a far cry from the deliberate scenes of poverty he produced during the 1850's, another example of which is a painting by the Belgian Alfred Stevens : *Ce qu'on appelle le vagabondage*.

Speaking on behalf of all those who rejected academic teachings, Castagnary, the chief theoretician of naturalism, wrote in his *Philosophie du Salon de 1857* : "Nature and man, portraiture and genre painting—in these lie the whole future of art" and boasted of "the free inspiration of the individual".

This free inspiration took the form of a search for a new way of painting, in which the matter would be visible, generously applied, and no longer mellow and smooth. All variations were possible and Jules Breton and Rosa Bonheur were immediately successful, like the advocates of naturalist orientalism, Fromentin and Guillaumet. But many others had a harder time of it ; Chintreuil, for example, was among the "Refusés" of 1863, but his great, light-filled painting *L'Espace* was finally admitted to the Luxembourg after the 1869 Salon. Provincial painters like Ravier, Monticelli and Guigou eked out their careers in relative isolation, only entering the Louvre at a far later date. The rapidly executed paintings of Carpeaux, known in his time as a successful sculptor, were unknown until 1906.

Portraiture was virtually excluded from the Luxembourg collections during the Second Empire. Even Carolus-Duran's *Dame au gant* which was exhibited at the 1869 Salon, was only acquired in 1875 when the artist had already achieved recognition. Like James Tissot's *Jeune femme en veste rouge*, which was shown at the 1864 Salon and acquired by the museum in 1907, the *Dame au gant* (a portrait of the painter's wife) is one of those pivotal works in which the artist shows what he is capable of doing if requested.

There is nothing surprising about the fact that the stars of the Salon des refusés of 1863 (Manet, Fantin-Latour and Whistler, an American who divided his time between London and Paris) did not gain admittance to the Luxembourg until about 1890. Indeed, Whistler's *Arrangement en gris et noir ; portrait de la mère de l'artiste* (painted in London in 1871 and exhibited in Paris in 1883) was sold to the museum for a token sum, for which the glory of admittance to the Luxembourg was probably ample compensation.

All these painters may be found in Fantin-Latour's *Hommage à Delacroix* composed just after Delacroix's death. They are carefully depicted alongside Champfleury, the defender of Courbet at the high point of realism a few years earlier ; and Baudelaire, whose intense admiration for Delacroix was tempered by shrewd judgement of the art of his time. Baudelaire had recognised the talent of Jongkind and, after meeting Eugène Boudin on the Normandy coast, publicised that painter's experiments in depicting the sky when he sent a canvas to the 1859 Salon. Boudin's formative influence on the young Claude Monet is well known.

Thus the strong personalities who were ill-treated by the official system and totally ignored by the Musée du Luxembourg were already united as a group, linked by ties of friendship and aesthetic affinity.

17

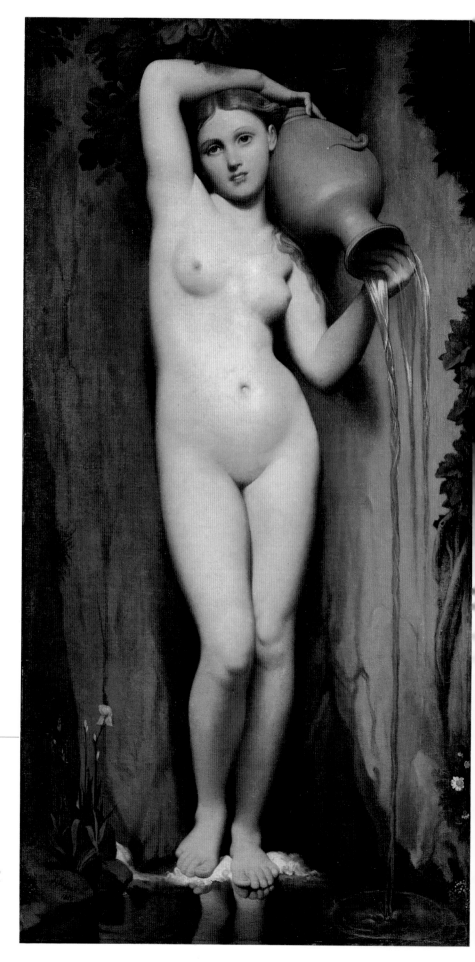

Jean Auguste Dominique Ingres (1780-1867)
La Source
Begun in Florence circa 1820,
completed in Paris in 1856
with the assistance of Paul Balze
and Alexandre Desgoffe
163 × 80
Bequest of countess Duchâtel, 1878

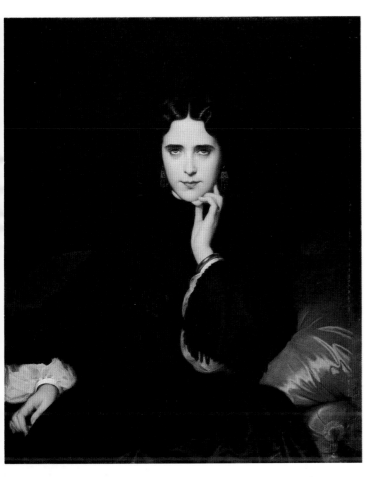

Amaury-Duval (1808-1885)
Madame de Loynes (1837-1908), 1862
1863 Salon
100 × 83
Bequest of Jules Lemaître, 1914

Jean-Léon Gerôme was twenty when he painted *Un combat de coqs*, which was one of the successes of the 1847 Salon. Nevertheless, Champfleury, the advocate of realism and promoter of what he called the Chalk School, reproached the young artist for having juxtaposed marble figures and fighting cocks " of flesh and blood, painted from nature''. Gerôme was a member of a neo-Grecian school (fervent admirers of Ingres) who painted fantasy and genre scenes inspired by Antiquity, using smooth techniques and studied perfection of line.

Jean-Léon Gérôme (1824-1904)
Jeunes Grecs faisant battre des coqs or *Un combat de coqs*, 1846
1847 Salon
143 × 204
Acquired in 1873

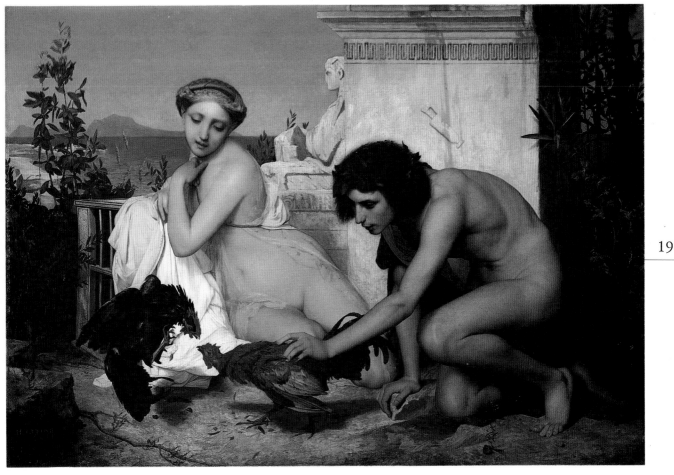

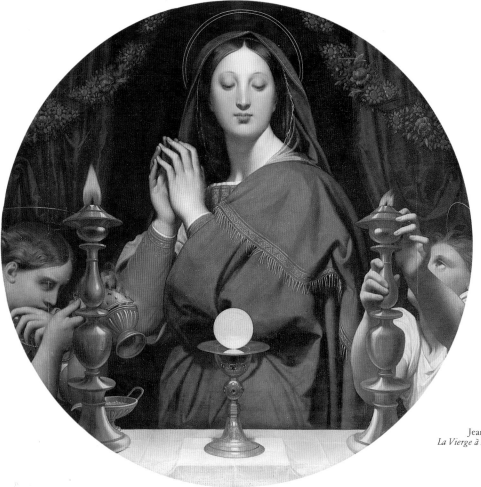

Jean Auguste Dominique Ingres (1780-1867)
La Vierge à l'hostie, 1854. Universal Exhibition of 1855
Diameter : 113
Commissioned in 1851

Jean-Léon Gérôme (1824-1904)
Jérusalem (La Crucifixion), 1867
82 × 144
Acquired in 1990

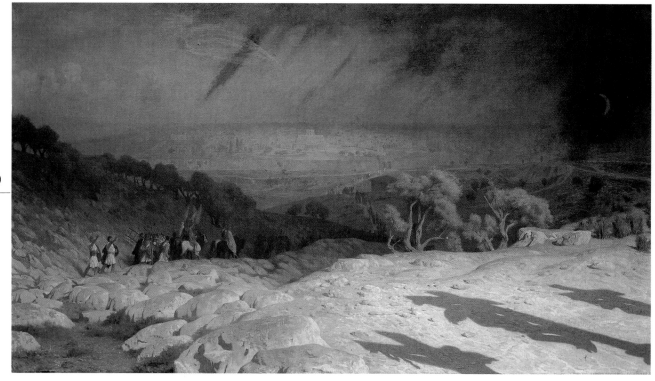

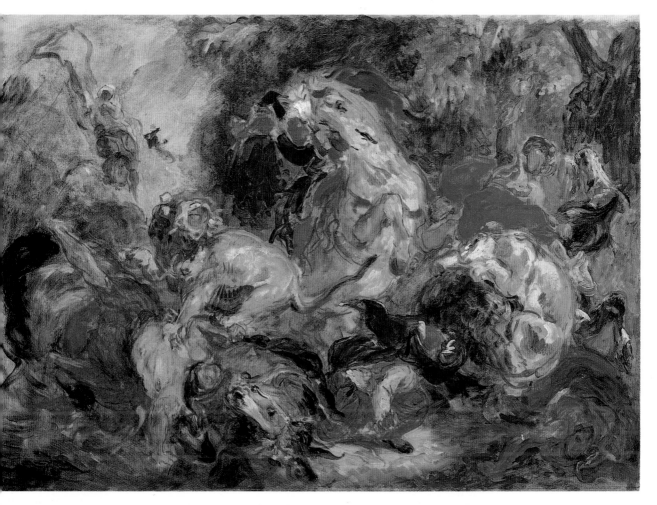

Eugène Delacroix (1798-1863)
Chasse aux lions, 1854
Sketch for a painting ordered by
the Musée de Bordeaux and exhibited at the 1855 Universal Exhibition
86 × 115
Acquired in 1984

21

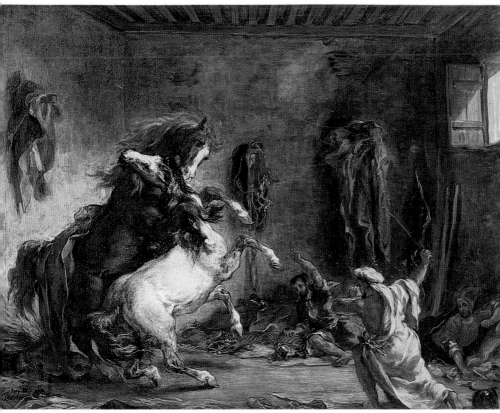

Eugène Delacroix (1798-1863)
*Chevaux arabes se battant dans
une écurie*, 1860
64,5 × 81
Bequest of count Isaac de
Camondo, 1911

In a décor inspired by plates from the Mazois collection on the *Ruines de Pompéi*, Chassériau here depicts a crowd of women who have come to rest and dry themselves after their bath, according to the Roman custom. However, in this *Tepidarium* the figures are languid, as in oriental scenes. To some extent, the work is Chassériau's response to romantic orientalism; for though he was a pupil of Ingres, he was also greatly attracted by the colours of Delacroix. One of the painting's chief assertions is that contemporary North Africa offered the spectacle of living Antiquity. Chassériau had visited Algeria in 1846 and his final work was to be the sketch for a projected *Intérieur de harem*.

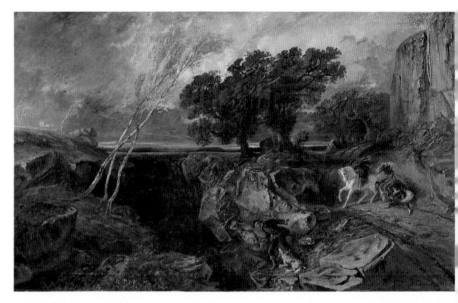

Paul Huet (1803-1869)
Le Gouffre, 1861 Salon
132 × 218
Acquired in 1985

Thomas Couture (1815-1879)
Romains de la décadence, 1847 Salon
472 × 772
Commissioned in 1846

22

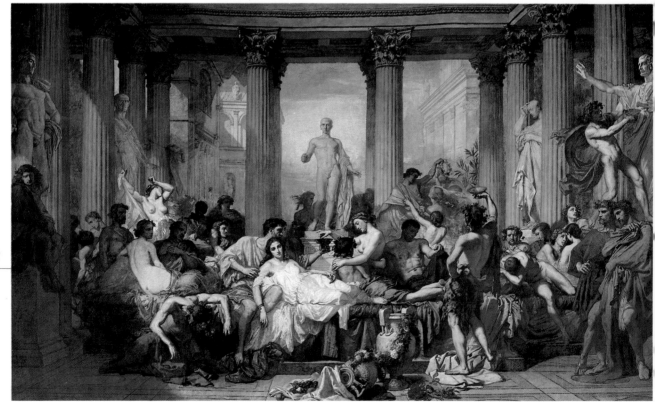

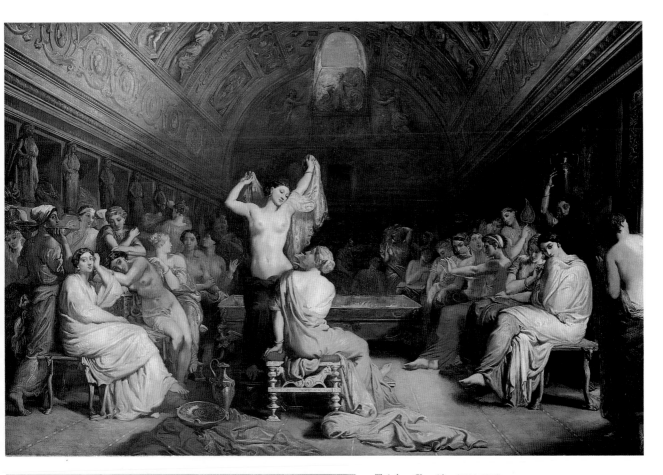

Théodore Chassériau (1819-1856)
Le Tépidarium
1853 Salon
171 × 258
Acquired in 1853

23

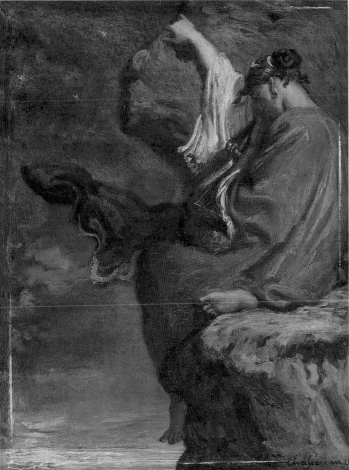

Théodore Chassériau (1819-1856)
Sapho, 1849. 1850-1851 Salon
27,5 × 21,5
Bequest of baron Arthur Chassériau, 1934

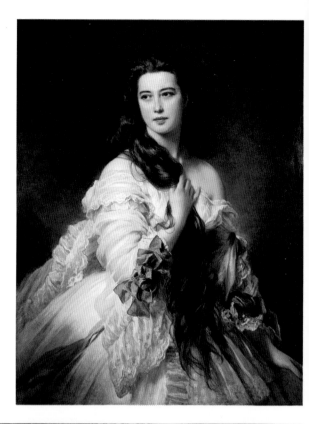

Franz-Xavier Winterhalter (1805 [?]-1873)
Mme Rimsky-Korsakov, 1864
117 × 90
Gift of Mme Rimsky-Korsakov, her sons, 1879

24

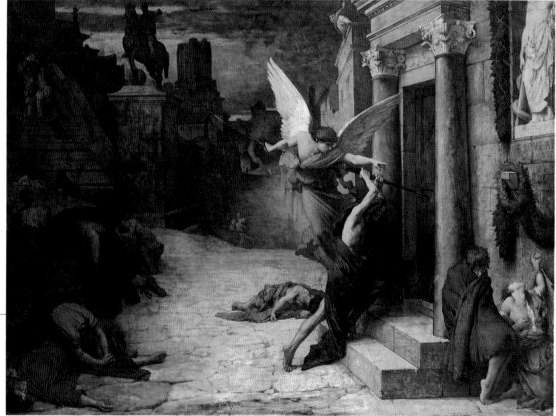

Elie Delaunay (1828-1891)
Peste à Rome (Jacopo da Voragine,
The Golden Legend, the legend of Saint Sebastian)
1869 Salon
131 × 176,5
Acquired in 1869

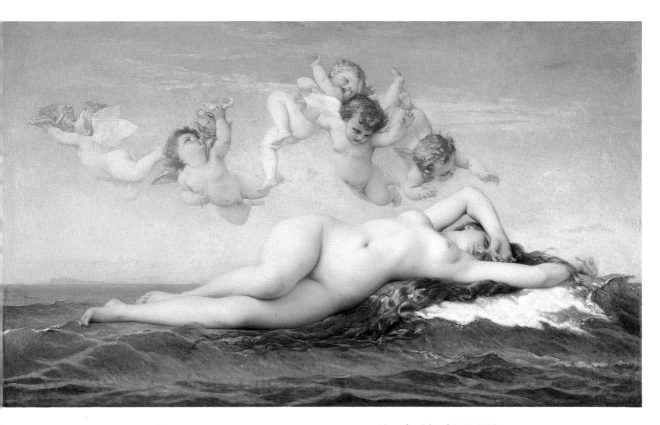

Alexandre Cabanel (1823-1889)
Naissance de Vénus, 1863 Salon
130 × 225
Purchased on Napoleon III's Civil List in 1863
and assigned to the National Museums in 1879

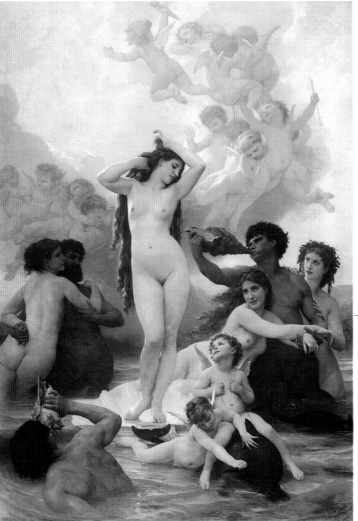

William Bouguereau (1825-1905)
Naissance de Vénus, 1879 Salon
300 × 218
Acquired in 1879

Both Bouguereau and Cabanel were pupils of Picot, the old professor at the Beaux-Arts who kept up the neo-classical tradition, and won the Prix de Rome; both had brilliant careers. Cabanel was elected to the Institute in the same year that his *Naissance de Vénus*, one of the key works of the 1863 Salon, was purchased by Napoleon III. In 1879, Bouguereau, who had already been a member of the Institute for three years, took up the oft-repeated theme of the birth of Venus, in this huge composition which displays all the stereotypes of contemporary academic art.

25

Henri Regnault (1843-1871)
Exécution sans jugement sous les rois maures de Grenade, 1870
302 × 146
Acquired in 1872

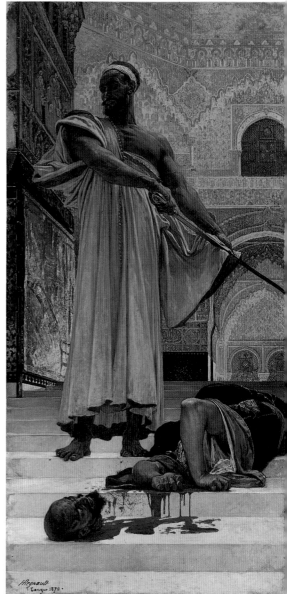

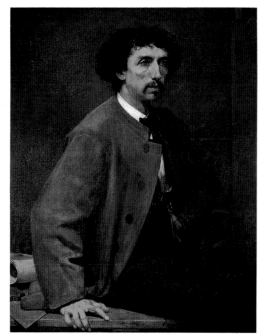

Paul Baudry (1828-1886)
Charles Garnier, architecte, 1868. 1869 Salon
103 × 81
Bequest of the widow of Charles Garnier to the château de
Versailles, 1922. Transferred to the Musée d'Orsay in 1986

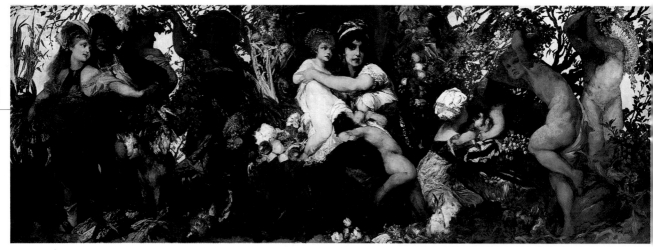

Hans Makart (1840-1884)
Abundantia : les dons de la terre, 1870
Painted for the dining-room of the Hoyos Palace
in Vienna, but never used
162,5 × 447
Acquired in 1973

R obert II, known as the Pious, son of Hugues Capet, had married Bertha of Burgundy while being godfather to one of her children from a former marriage. This relationship made their union incestuous in the eyes of the church. Pope Gregory V excommunicated the king while he refused to repudiate his wife. Jean-Paul Laurens used the perspective of the throne room to portray the condemned couple in dramatic isolation. The artist, who had met Manet at the Salon des refusés in 1863, kept faith with the historical subject he had chosen out of his own conviction. Deeply atheistic, he in effect condemned the religious fanaticism of the church.

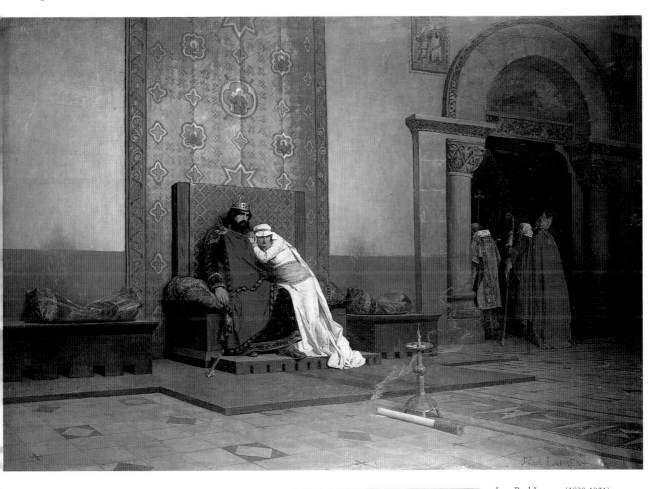

Jean-Paul Laurens (1838-1921)
L'Excommunication de Robert le Pieux
1875 Salon
130 × 218
Purchased in 1875

27

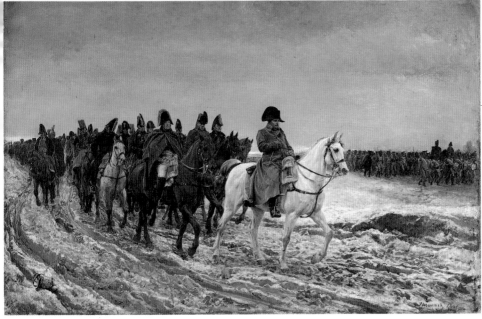

Ernest Meissonier (1815-1891)
Campagne de France, 1814
1864 Salon
51,5 × 76,5
Bequest of Alfred Chauchard, 1909

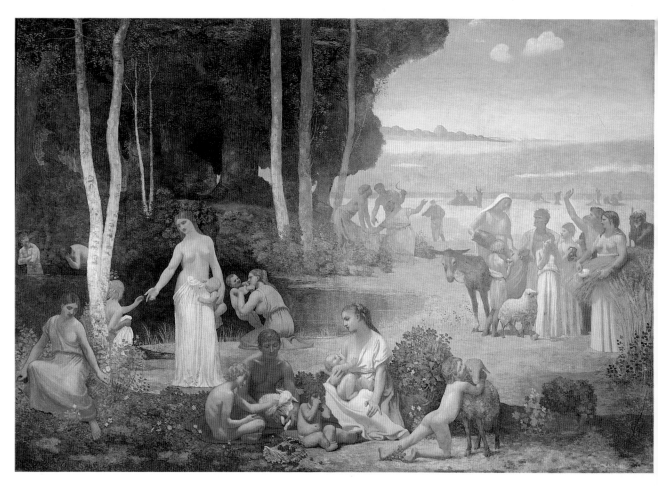

Pierre Puvis de Chavannes (1824-1898)
L'Été, 1873 Salon
350 × 507
Acquired by the State in 1873, for the Musée de Chartres
admitted to the Musée d'Orsay in 1985

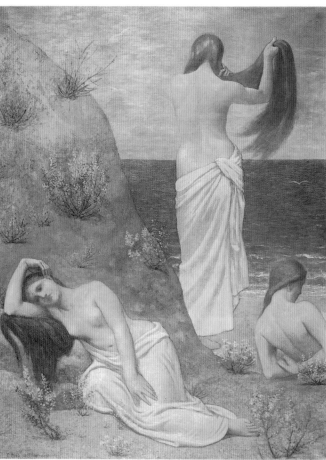

Pierre Puvis de Chavannes (1824-1898)
Jeunes filles au bord de la mer (decorative panel)
1879 Salon
205 × 154
Gift of Robert Gérard, 1970

uvis de Chavannes was a specialist in monumental painting. His
flat technique, without shadows or reliefs, in clear tints matching
the stone of the wall surfaces on which he usually worked, may also be found
in his smaller pictures. *Le Pauvre pêcheur* was shown in the 1881 Salon and
frequently re-exhibited until 1887 when it was purchased for the Musée du
Luxembourg. It had an immediate fascination for younger artists like Seurat
and Maillol, and confirmed Puvis as one of the forerunners of symbolism by
its striking new images. All the elements of the composition, even the mast
leaning toward the left, unite to create a special vision of poverty.

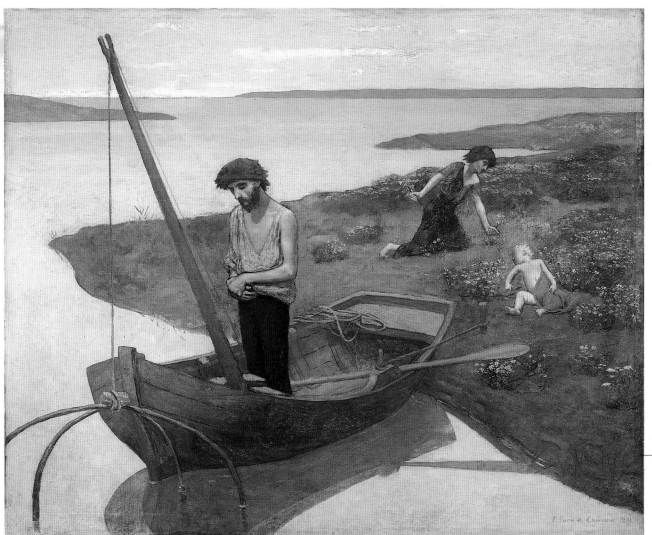

Pierre Puvis de Chavannes (1824-1898)
Le Pauvre pêcheur, 1881 Salon
155,5 × 192,5
Acquired in 1887

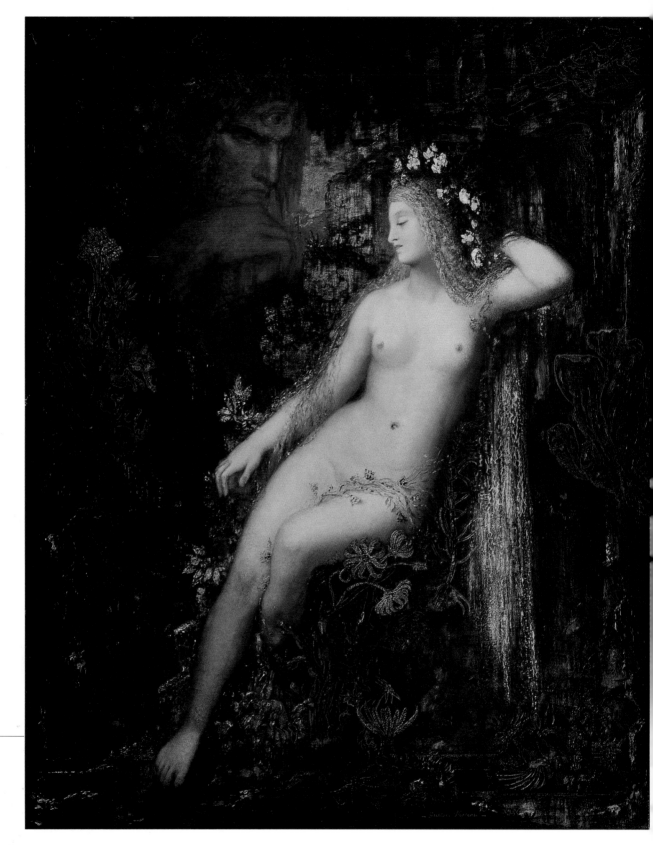

30

Gustave Moreau (1826-1898)
Galatée, 1880-1881
85,5 x 66
Acquired with the help of the Fondation Philippe Meyer
and a syndicate of Japanese artlovers coordinated
by the *Nikkei* daily newspaper, and the participation
of the Fonds du Patrimoine in 1997

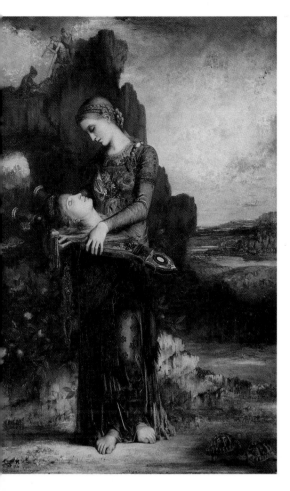

It was under the influence of Gustave Moreau whom he had met in Italy in 1857 that Degas as a young man first became interested in painting based on antique subjects. On his return to France Moreau slowly prepared a few history pictures for the Salon. In 1866, his poetic vision of the young Thracian girl carrying the head of Orphens already heralded Symbolism. At the Salon of 1880 the nymph Galatea (*Galatée*) spied on by the cyclops Polyphemus was hailed as a masterpiece on a par with the works of the Renaissance. It inspired J.K. Huysmans to write a famous passage, praising « the magian effects wrought by the brush of this visionary » and describing the marine cave as a « cavern light up by precious stones like a tabernacle, and containing the inimitable radiant jewel, the white body of Galatea, tinged with pink on her breasts and lips, asleep amidst her long, pale tresses! »

Gustave Moreau (1826-1898)
Orphée, 1865. 1866 Salon
154 x 99,5
Acquired in 1866

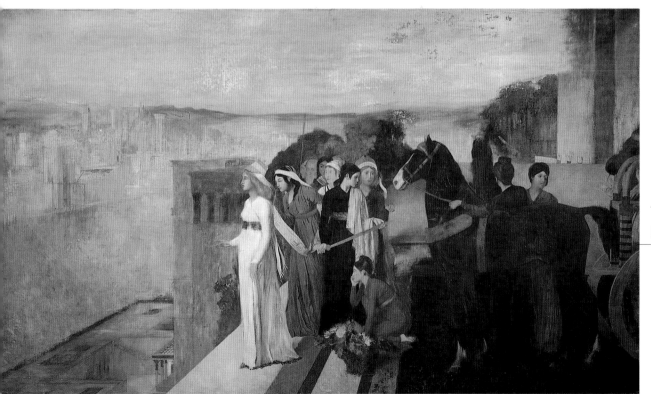

31

Edgar Degas (1834-1917)
Sémiramis construisant Babylone, 1861
151 × 258
Acquired in 1918

Honoré Daumier (1808-1879)
La Blanchisseuse, circa 1863
49 × 33,5
Acquired with the assistance of
D. David-Weill, 1927

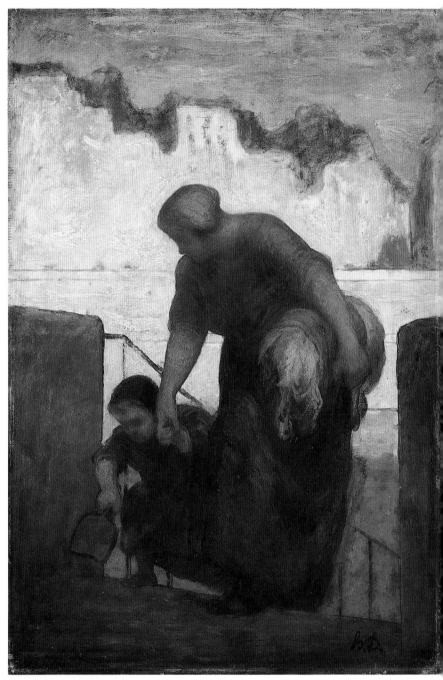

Honoré Daumier (1808-1879)
Crispin et Scapin, circa 1864
60,5 × 82
Gift of the Société des Amis du Louvre
with the assistance of the successors
of Henri Rouart, 1912

32

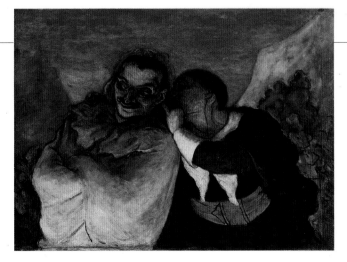

Théodore Rousseau (1812-1867)
Clairière dans la haute futaie, known as *La Charette*
1863 Salon
28 × 53
Bequest of Alfred Chauchard, 1909

Narcisse Diaz de la Peña (1807-1876)
Les Hauteurs du Jean de Paris
(forest of Fontainebleau), 1867
86 × 106
Bequest of Alfred Chauchard, 1909

Jules Dupré (1811-1889)
La Vanne, circa 1855-1860
51 × 69
Bequest of Alfred Chauchard, 1909

Well in advance of Pont-Aven or Saint-Tropez, a small country village named Barbizon, on the edge of the forest of Fontainebleau, had become famous as a haunt of artists. After 1820, painters like Diaz and Théodore Rousseau settled there, whilst others of every tendency would come to spend the summer months. 1849 saw the arrival of Millet and Charles Jacque. Jules Dupré was an occasional visitor, though he preferred other wooded areas in the Ile de France. The school of Barbizon was specifically composed of painters who made a rule of direct observation of nature and light. Their works served as a point of departure for the experiments of younger artists like Monet and his friends.

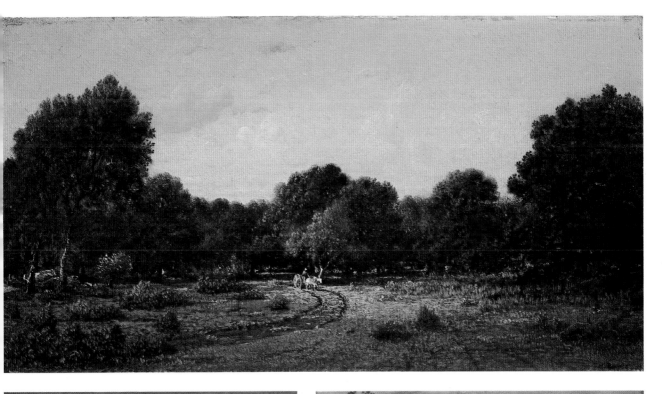

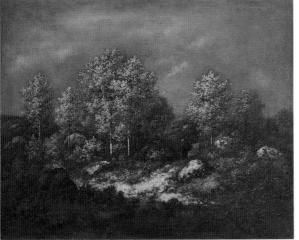

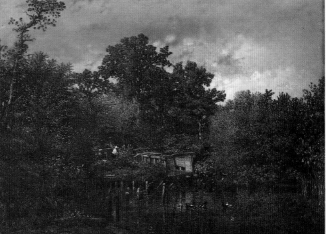

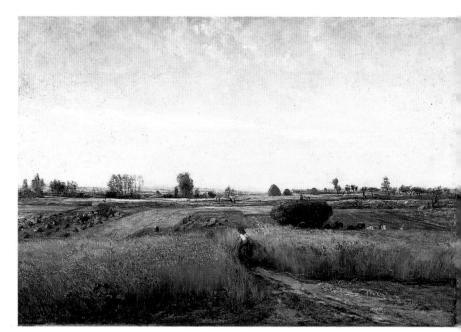

Charles Daubigny (1817-1878)
La Moisson, 1851. 1852 Salon
135 × 196
Acquired in 1853

Jean-François Millet (1814-1875)
Les Glaneuses, 1857 Salon
83,5 × 111
Gift of Mme Pommery, 1890

34

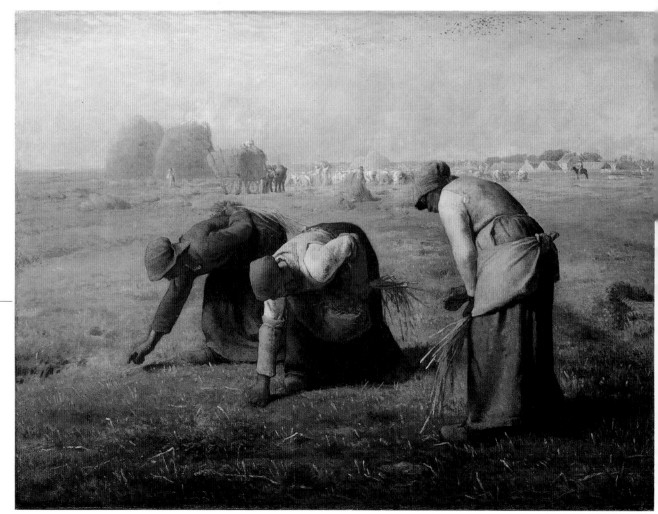

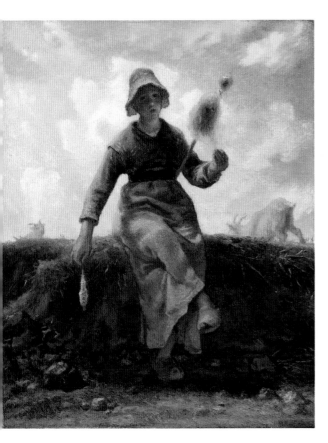

L'*Angélus* acquired enduring fame in the early years of the Third Republic and Millet, only a few years after his death, was seen as the epitome of the peasant-painter. At the time of the Secrétan sale in 1889, when *L'Angélus* was sold for a record price, innumerable reproductions of it had already been made and distributed throughout the world. This success was confirmed by exhibitions organised in the USA, before it was bought back in 1890 by the Parisian collector Alfred Chauchard, who left it to the Louvre.

Jean-François Millet (1814-1875)
La Fileuse, chevrière auvergnate, 1868-1869
92,5 × 73,5
Bequest of Alfred Chauchard, 1909

Jean-François Millet (1814-1875)
L'Angélus, 1857-1859
55,5 × 66
Bequest of Alfred Chauchard, 1909

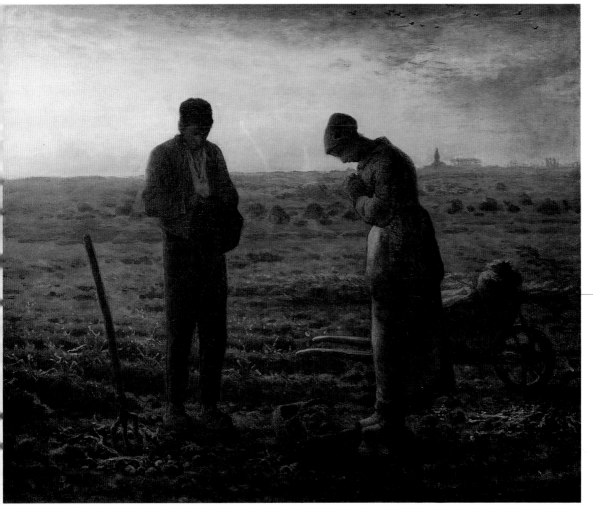

35

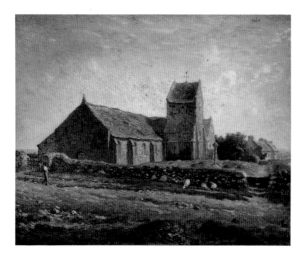

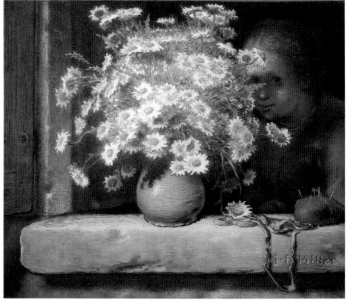

Jean-François Millet (1814-1875)
Le Printemps, 1868-1873
86 × 111
Gift of Mme Frédéric Hartmann, 1887

36

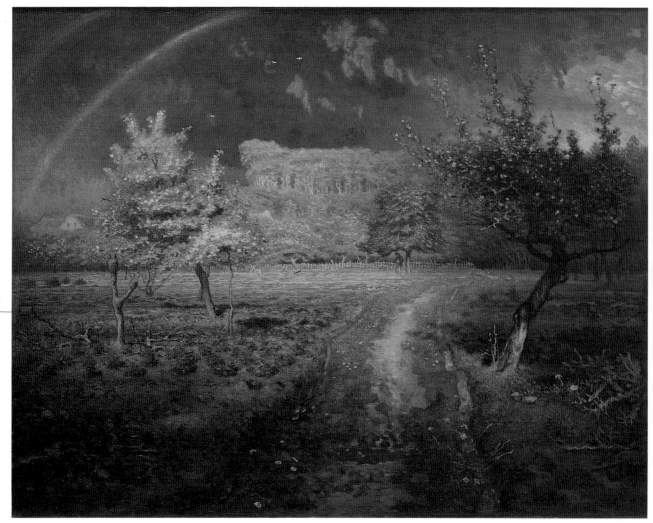

Jean-François Millet (1814-1875)
L'Église de Gréville, 1871-1874
60 × 73,5
Acquired at a posthumous auction
of the artist's works, 1875

Jean-François Millet (1814-1875)
Le Bouquet de marguerites, 1871-1874
Pastel on beige paper, 68 × 83
Acquired on arrears of the Dol-Lair
bequest, 1949

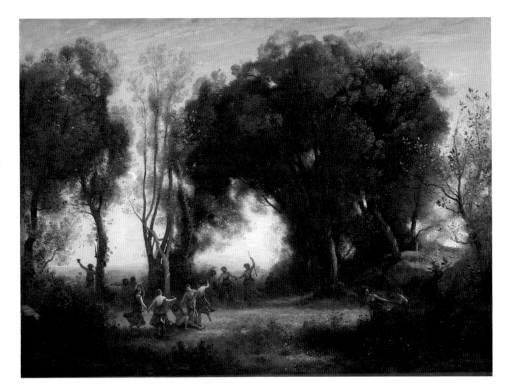

Jean-Baptiste Camille Corot (1796-1875)
Une matinée. La Danse des nymphes
1850-1851 Salon
98 × 131
Acquired in 1851

Jean-Baptiste Camille Corot (1796-1875)
L'Atelier de Corot, circa 1865-1870
56 × 46
Acquired in 1933

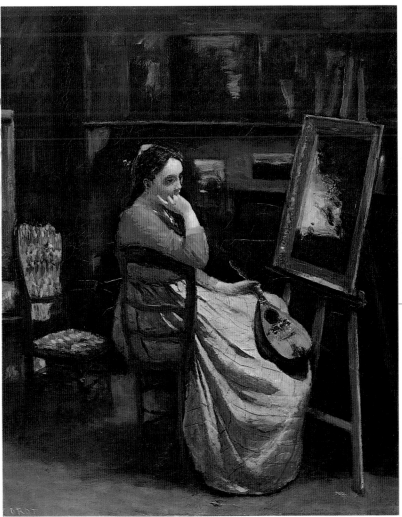

37

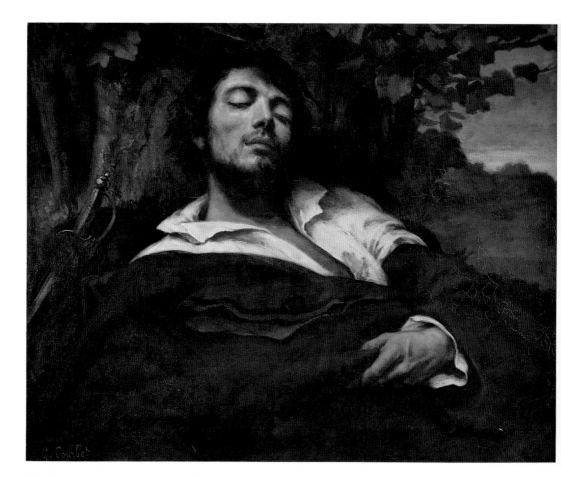

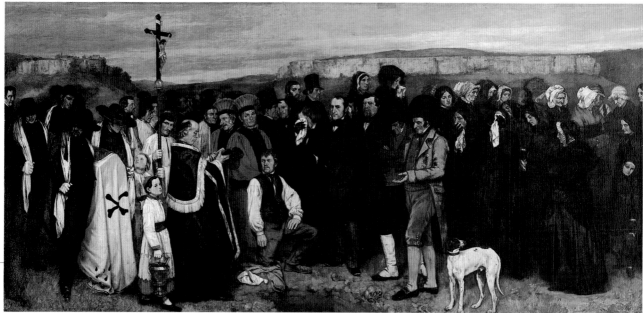

Gustave Courbet (1819-1877)
L'Homme blessé, 1844
81,5 × 97,5
Acquired on the sale of the artist's studio, 1881

Gustave Courbet (1819-1877)
Un enterrement à Ornans, 1849-1850. 1850-1851 Salon
315 × 668
Gift of Mlle Juliette Courbet, 1881

ourbet, emboldened by his success at the 1849 Salon, in December of that year began executing on canvas his immense composition *Un enterrement à Ornans*. During the autumn he had sketched over fifty inhabitants of his native village for the work, which was his first painting on a monumental scale. The aim was to depict a banal and familiar occurrence, the country funeral of an unknown person, using the same format as that of historical painting and lifesize figures. Courbet's inspiration here seems to have come from Spanish art and the great collective portraits of 17th-century Holland; but *Un enterrement à Ornans* is also a proof of his stern realism, even when dealing with such a sacred subject as death.

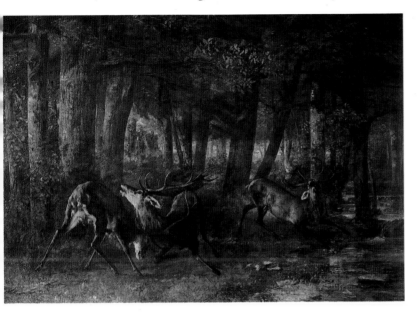

Gustave Courbet (1819-1877)
Le Rut du printemps. Combat de cerfs, 1861 Salon
355 × 507
Acquired on the sale of the artist's studio, 1881

Gustave Courbet (1819-1877)
L'Atelier du peintre. Allégorie réelle, 1855
361 × 598
Acquired by public subscription, with the aid
of the Société des Amis du Louvre, 1920

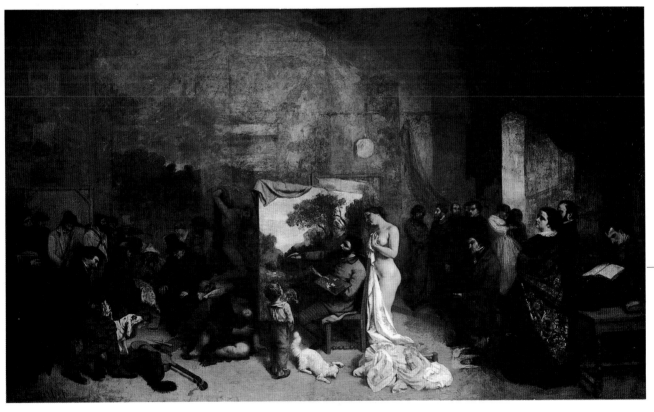

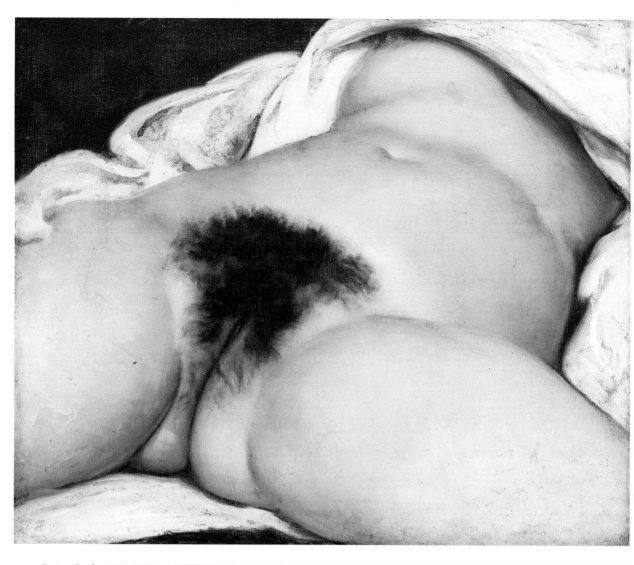

Gustave Courbet (1819-1877)
L'Origine du Monde, 1866
46 x 55
Acquired through dation in 1995

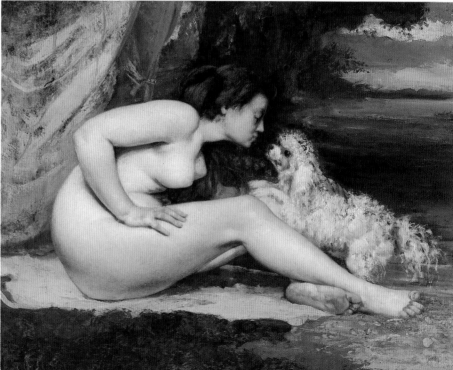

Gustave Courbet (1819-1877)
Femme nue au chien, 1861-1862
later dated 1868
65 × 81
Acquired by dation 1979

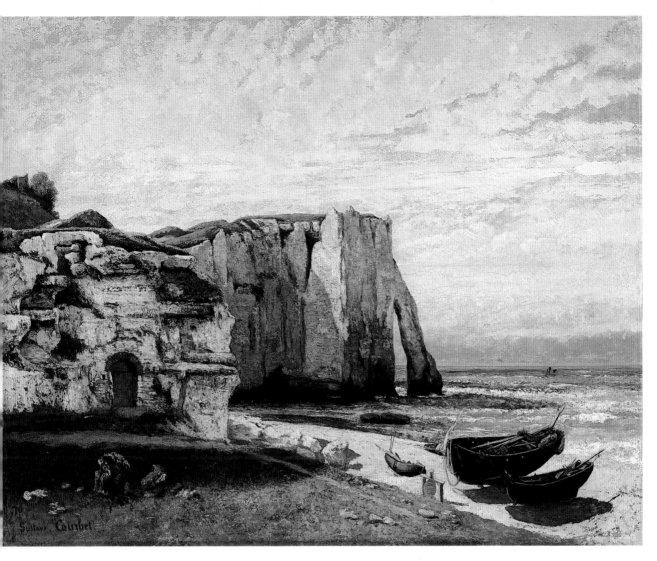

Gustave Courbet (1819-1877)
La Falaise d'Étretat après l'orage, 1870 Salon
133 × 162
Assigned by the Office des biens privés, 1950

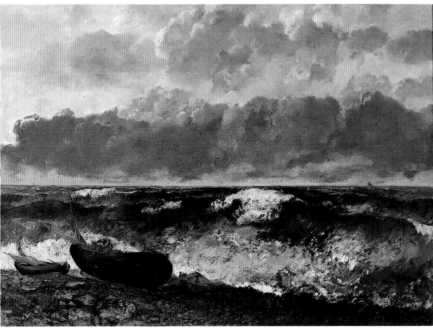

Gustave Courbet (1819-1877)
La Mer orageuse or *La Vague*, 1870 Salon
117 × 150,5
Acquired in 1878

Two years after Millet had caused a scandal with his *Glaneuses*, who were viewed as the "three fates of pauperism", Jules Breton presented *Le Rappel des glaneuses* at the 1859 Salon. The painting was a success, its figures described as "beautiful, rustic caryatids". It is true that Breton, who considered himself one of the pioneers of country realist painting, applied himself to scenes of everyday life in his native village of Courrières, like Courbet at Ornans or Millet at Barbizon. But his approach was different, with more of a narrative slant. Later Jules Breton established himself as the official artist of life in the fields.

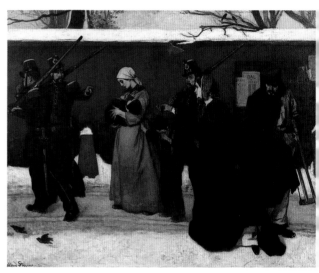

Alfred Stevens (1823-1906)
Ce qu'on appelle le vagabondage
Universal Exhibition 1855
132 × 162
Bequest of Léon Lhermitte, 1926

42

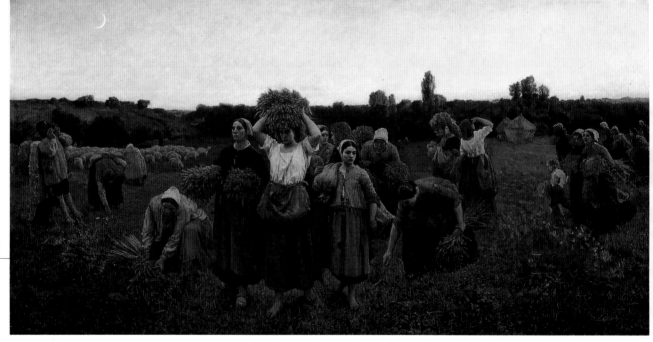

Jules Breton (1827-1906)
Le Rappel des glaneuses, 1859 Salon
90 × 176
Acquired on Napoléon III's Civil List in 1859
and given to the Imperial Museum in 1862

Rosa Bonheur (1822-1899)
Labourage nivernais ; le sombrage
1849 Salon
134 × 260
Commissioned by the State, 1848

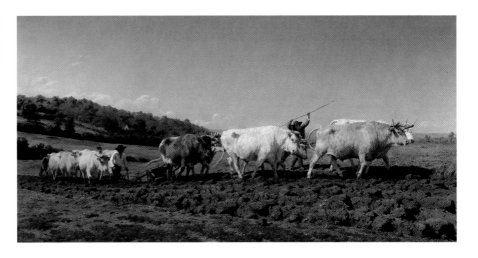

Antoine Chintreuil (1814-1873)
L'Espace, 1869 Salon
102 × 202
Acquired in 1869

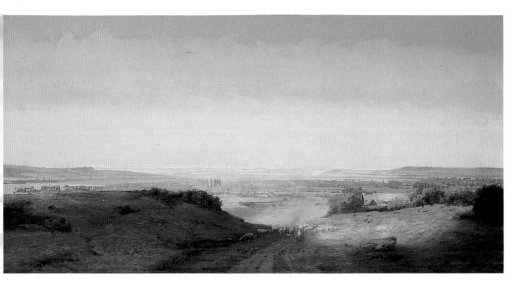

Charles-François Daubigny
(1817-1878)
La Neige, 1873
90 × 120
Acquired by dation in 1989

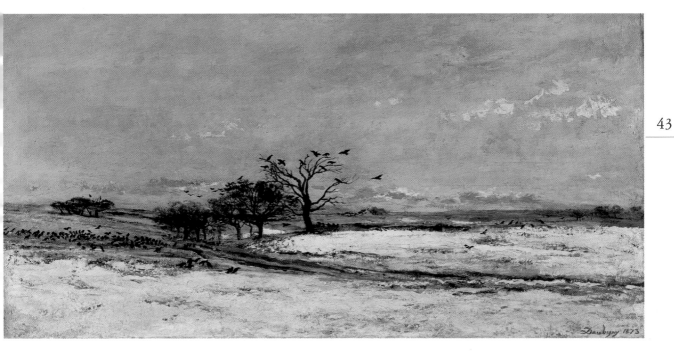

Eugène Fromentin (1820-1876)
Chasse au faucon en Algérie : la curée, 1863 Salon
162 × 118
Acquired in 1863

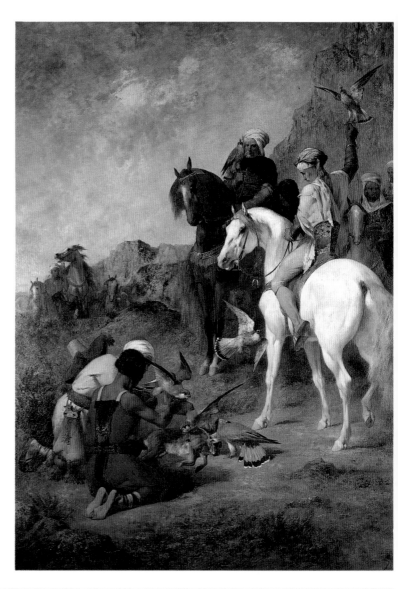

Gustave Guillaumet (1840-1887)
Le Sahara, or *Le Désert*, 1867. 1868 Salon
110 × 200
Gift of the artist's family, 1888

44

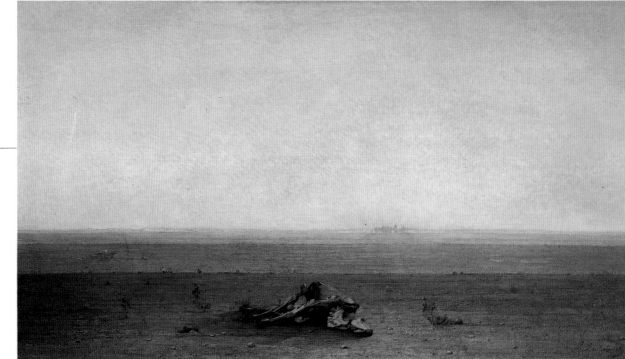

Jean-Baptiste Carpeaux (1827-1875)
L'Attentat de Berezowski (6 June, 1867), 1867
130 × 195
Acquired on the sale of the artist's studio, 1906

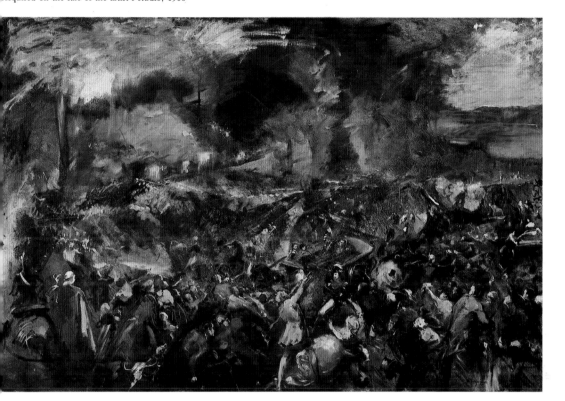

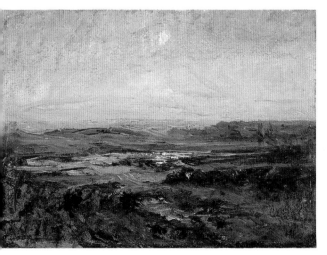

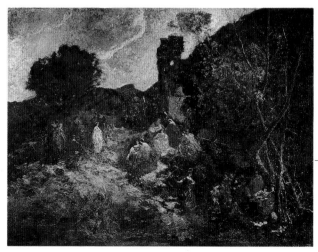

45

Auguste Ravier (1814-1895)
L'Étang de la Levaz, à Morestel (Isère)
24,8 × 33,5
Gift of Félix Thiollier, 1909

Adolphe-Joseph Monticelli (1824-1886)
Don Quichotte et Sancho Pança, 1865
96,5 × 130
Acquired on arrears of an anonymous Canadian donation, 1953

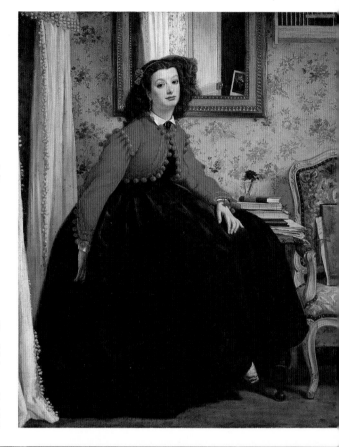

Paradoxically, it is the sage Fantin-Latour, with his austere collective portraits in the tradition of the Dutch masters, who has left us the image of the most revolutionary literary and artistic groups of the day. His first great composition, *Hommage à Delacroix* (presented at the 1864 Salon), included Fantin himself with his friends, Whistler, Manet and Baudelaire (seated far right) around Delacroix' self-portrait. In *Coin de table* (1872), note the presence of Verlaine and Rimbaud (at left).

46

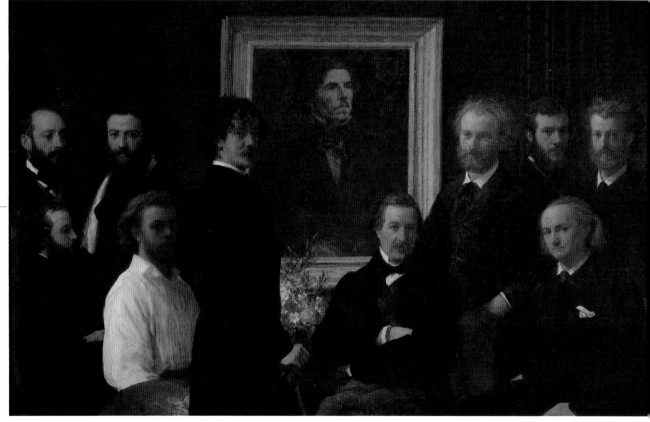

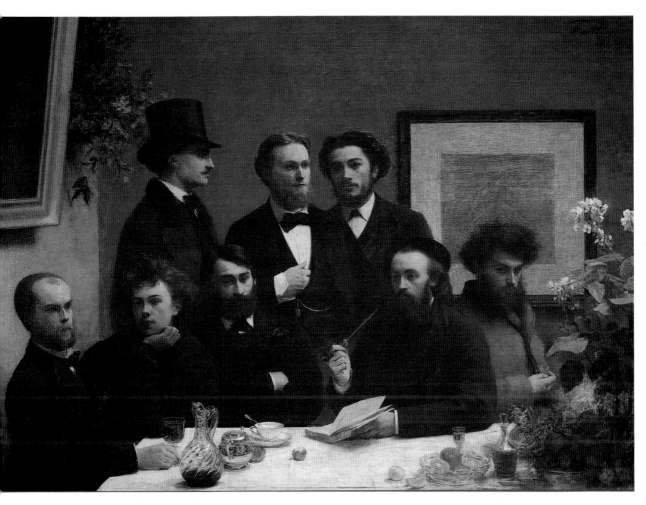

47

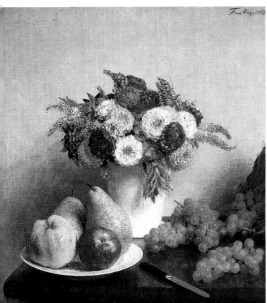

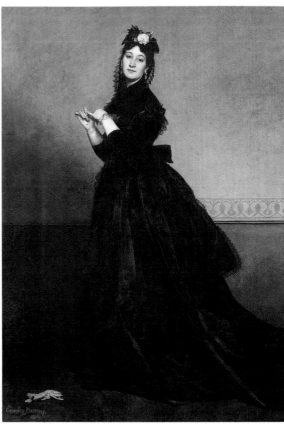

Henri Fantin-Latour (1836-1904)
Fleurs et Fruits, 1865
74 × 57
Ceded by l'Office des biens privés, 1950

Carolus-Duran (1838-1917)
La Dame au gant, 1869 Salon
228 × 164
Acquired in 1875

anet's composition (the first he exhibited at any Salon, that of 1861 owes much to Courbet's influence. Nonetheless, it already reveals the broad, honest skill of the young artist, along with his original way of handling space by simplifying planes. The Degas painting, done at roughly the same time, displays similar preoccupations; this portrait, which represents the wife of the artist and his family when they were living in Florence, is a reminder of Degas' connection with Italy and his travels there as a young man. Whistler too was attached to Courbet at the start of his career, but he was later influenced by the art of Japan, like many of his contemporaries.

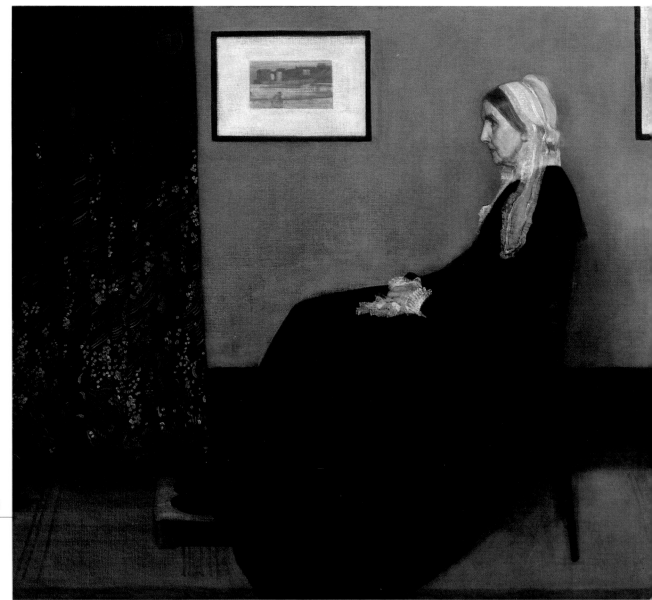

James McNeill Whistler (1834-1903)
Arrangement en gris et noir or *The Artist's Mother*, 187
1883 Salo
144 × 16
Acquired in 189

48

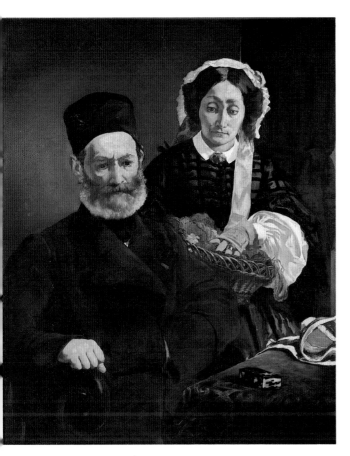

Édouard Manet (1832-1883)
Monsieur et Madame Auguste Manet, *les parents de l'artiste*, 1860
1861 Salon
110 × 90
Acquired through the generosity of the Rouart-Manet family
Mme Jeannette Veil-Picard and an anonymous foreign donor, 1977

Edgar Degas (1834-1917)
Portrait de Famille. La famille Bellelli, begun in 1858
1867 Salon
200 × 250
Acquired in 1918, by agreement with count and countess de Fels
with the cooperation of René de Gas

49

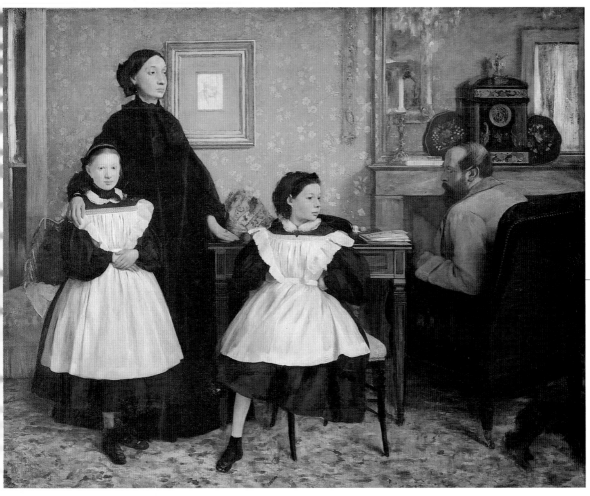

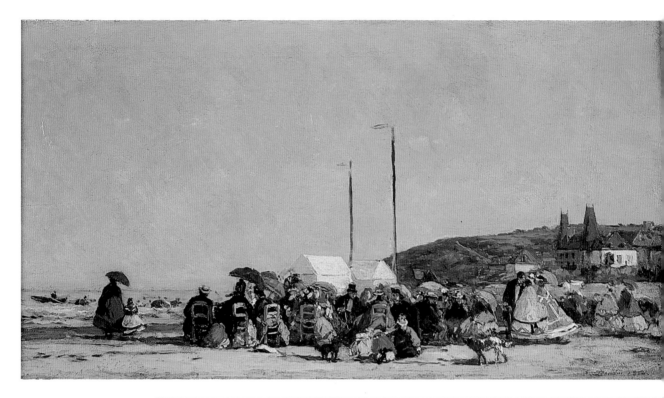

Eugène Boudin (1824-1898)
La Plage de Trouville, 1864
26 × 48
Gift of Dr Eduardo Mollard
1961

50

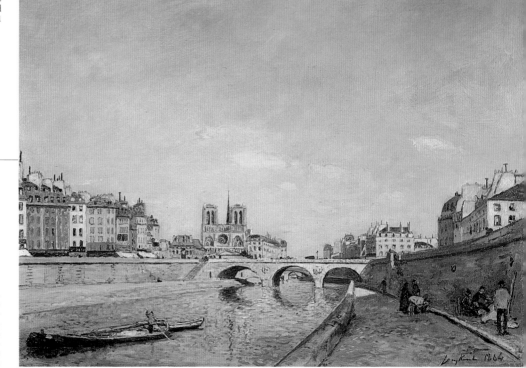

Johan-Barthold Jongkind
(1819-1891)
*La Seine et Notre-Dame
de Paris*, 1864
42 × 56
Bequest of Enriqueta Alsop
in the name
of Dr Eduardo Mollard, 1972

Paul Guigou (1834-1871)
Lavandière, 1860
81 × 59
Gift of Paul Rosenberg, 1912

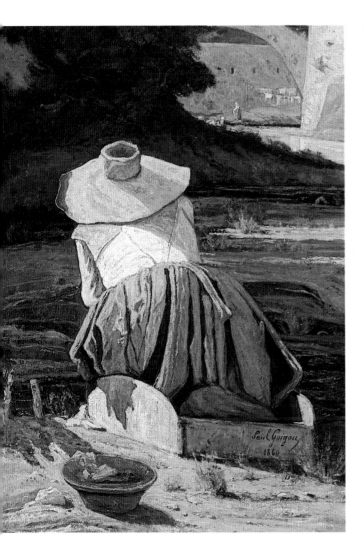

Stanislas Lépine (1835-1892)
Paysage, 1869
30 × 58,5
Bequest of Enriqueta Alsop, in the name
of Dr Eduardo Mollard, in 1972

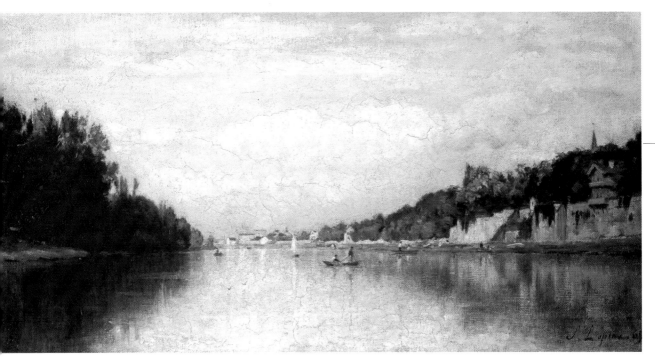

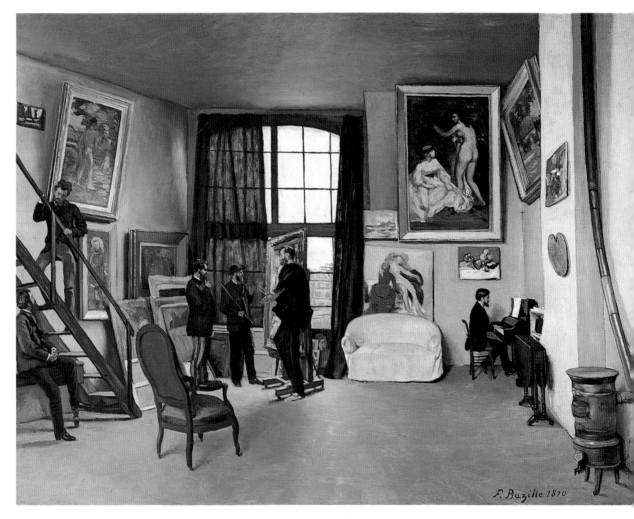

Frédéric Bazille (1841-1870
L'Atelier de Bazille rue de la Condamine, 187●
98 × 12●
Bequest of Marc Bazille, the artist's brother, 192●

52

Impressionism

Fantin-Latour was an habitué of the Café Guerbois, which was the scene of many a violent discussion between the future impressionists and their critics. His huge 1870 canvas *L'Atelier des Batignolles* shows the avant-garde of French painting, Renoir, Bazille and Monet, gathered in the café around Manet. All three had studied in the highly academic Gleyre studio; nonetheless, they were passionate emulators of the man who painted *Le Déjeuner sur l'herbe*. With them, Fantin-Latour depicted their supporters, Edmond Maître, Zacharie Astruc and Zola, critics who had taken a brave public stand in preferring their work to that of the stars of the contemporary Salon. With its fine classical treatment, which doubtless smoothed the way for its acquisition by the Musée du Luxembourg in 1892, this great painting serves as a counterpoint to the *Hommage à Delacroix* of a few years earlier, in showing the state of the painting avant-garde just before the upheavals of the war of 1870 and the Commune. Manet, the uncontested leader, was ''a man of great modesty and gentleness'', in Zola's phrase; but he was also highly energetic and ambitious, and this, coupled with the daring of his art, explains the influence he wielded over painters like Monet, Renoir and Bazille, who were not very much younger than he.

The same group appears in a much more relaxed canvas by Bazille dating from the same time, depicting the latter's atelier in the rue de la Condamine. Bazille, a native of Montpellier from a well-to-do background, had arrived in Paris in 1862 as a young man and had immediately made friends with Monet and Renoir. All the same, the principles used in this free evocation of Bazille's studio are those of Manet; on the walls are Bazille's most recent canvases, among them his *Nude* in the process of being painted. This picture, entitled *La Toilette*, was refused admittance to the 1870 Salon; this was the occasion of Bazille's last public appearance, since he volunteered shortly afterward for the army and was tragically killed in battle at Beaune-la-Rollande the same year. In 1870, Bazille's painting was typical of the ambiguous and uncomfortable position of many another future impressionist; their style of painting was acceptable but they were repeatedly refused entry to the Salon. Hence they were not yet ready to give up trying, and sometimes they succeeded in persuading the jury to admit them.

This was not Manet's case in 1863. The historic rejection of his *Déjeuner sur l'herbe* by the Salon of that year (along with innumerable works by other artists such as Whistler, Cazin and Pissarro) caused a general outcry in the painting establishment. Recognising this, the Emperor Napoleon III authorized the ''Refusés'' to exhibit their paintings under Manet's banner in rooms adjacent to the Salon: hence the name Salon des refusés. *Le Déjeuner sur l'herbe* was the star of this alternative Salon and attracted a hail of sarcasm from the public and critics. In the real Salon, the Venuses of Cabanel, Baudry and Amaury-Duval were extravagantly praised, and the Emperor himself purchased Cabanel's picture for the Luxembourg. Manet's *Déjeuner sur l'herbe* remained for twenty years in his studio, before being bought by the singer Faure, then the great dealer Durand-Ruel. It finally came into the hands of Moreau-Nélaton just before 1900, and it is to this brilliant collector that we owe the entry of Manet's masterpiece to the Louvre in 1907. In the same year, *Olympia*, which had been offered to the State in 1890, produced another armed rising when the decision was made to hang it in the Louvre beside Ingres' *Grande Odalisque*.

Both *Le Déjeuner sur l'herbe* and *Olympia* are based on classical art. Titian's *Concert champêtre* (Louvre), and an engraving from the school of Raphael, were the sources for the *Déjeuner*; while Titian's *Venus of Urbino* (Florence, Uffizi) and Goya's *Maja desnuda* (Madrid, Prado) inspired *Olympia*. Manet's apparent lack of deference to his predecessors and his resolutely modern interpretation profoundly shocked the public. Rare indeed were the critics like Zola and Astruc, who were capable of recognising Manet's genius for fresh treatment of traditional subjects and daring method of painting *par taches* (in patches). "Manet! One of the greatest artistic characters of our time", wrote Astruc in 1863. As for Zola, after a spirited defence of both paintings, he went on to write an article that aroused world-wide interest in 1867, entitled "A new way of painting : Edouard Manet". The following year, the painter paid Zola the tribute of painting his portrait, with *Olympia* in the background beside a Japanese print which testifies to the growing fascination of contemporary artists with the art of Japan.

The Manet collection at the Musée d'Orsay, which is mostly composed of the gifts and bequests of Caillebotte, Moreau-Nélaton and Camondo, is indicative of the highs and lows of the painter's career. He continued calmly to submit his work to the test of the Salon, unmoved by historic rebuffs like that of *Le Déjeuner sur l'herbe* or *Le Fifre*, or even by triumphs like that of *Le Balcon*, a portrait of his friend Berthe Morisot which was admitted in 1869. Manet's development is clearly perceptible from the bluntly realist style of *Les Parents de l'artiste* (acquired in 1977) to later works stamped by the influence of the impressionist techniques that he himself had helped to create (*Sur la plage*, *La Blonde aux Seins Nus*).

Monet's *Déjeuner sur l'herbe* was a direct response to Manet. This painting was quickly followed by *Femmes au jardin*, another large canvas with Camille Doncieux, who was to become Monet's wife in 1870, among its figures. According to a friend of Monet, *Femmes au jardin* was "begun in the open air and painted from life", quite an accomplishment in view of its size. The work was refused admittance to the 1867 Salon, and although to some extent it reflects Manet's influence, its main interest is in the light it casts on the experiments of Monet himself : namely, the preservation, in the completed work, of the vivacity inherent in the sketch, the blending of figures into surrounding space by an energetic interplay of shadow and light, and the whole composition painted with broad juxtaposed strokes.

Thematic and open air painting were at the heart of the impressionist initiative, from the first experiments of Monet and Boudin, to the work of Courbet on the Normandy coast. The open air was crucial to their doctrine, and became a principle of composition intimately linked to the development of a pictorial technique which sought to render the spontaneity of the perceived impression by way of the subject's variations according to light. In this context, the technique generated a style and then a whole philosophy of the act of painting; this Monet was to push to its outer limits with his famous sequence of paintings, represented at the Musée d'Orsay by *Les Meules*, the five *Cathédrales de Rouen* and *Nymphéas bleus*. In this regard, the impressionist collection offers a particularly striking demonstration of the implications of open air painting, since it is mainly composed of landscapes of the great impressionist shrines of the Normandy coast (*L'Hôtel des Roches Noires*), Argenteuil (*Régates*), Pontoise (*Les Toits rouges*), Auvers-sur-Oise, Vétheuil, Eragny and Giverny. The acquisition of *La Pie* in 1985 added a masterpiece to an already impressive series. Monet probably painted this in January or February 1869 during a stay in the Etretat region, and its stunning variations of white show the painter's extraordinary scrutiny of light effects and above all his great technical mastery.

After the 1870 war, which had dispersed them widely, the group gathered once again around Monet, who went to live at Argenteuil on the banks of the Seine around 1871. Here, Monet, Renoir, Sisley and later Manet came to paint the same subjects, immortalising in a series of wonderfully fresh canvases the regattas at Argenteuil, and the marina with its two bridges. This golden age of impressionism is abundantly represented at the Musée d'Orsay by paintings from the Caillebotte bequest, the Moreau-Nélaton gift and the Personnaz and Camondo bequests. Monet's famous *Coquelicots* was also painted at Argenteuil; this picture figured in the first impressionist exhibition of 1874, and was echoed by Renoir's *Chemin montant dans les hautes herbes*.

Having produced heavily-structured landscapes of the Pontoise region such as *Le Coteau de l'Hermitage, Pontoise* (which recently entered the Orsay collection as the result of a dation), Pissarro adopted a more fluid manner with his famous *Gelée blanche* and *Les Toits rouges*, which were featured in the impressionist exhibitions of 1874 and 1877. The museum also possesses a fine self-portrait by this artist, and he is otherwise well represented by forty or so paintings from every stage of his long career, chiefly thanks to the Personnaz bequest of 1937. Fourteen canvases painted at Louveciennes, Pontoise and finally Eragny, where the artist settled in 1884, show the development of his technique from its beginnings right up to the pointilliste phase between 1886-88 and beyond. *La Vue du pont de Rouen* also shows that Pissarro could be an excellent painter of town scenes, and that he was acutely aware of the environmental changes that were taking place under the pressure of industrial development.

While Pissarro played a prominent role as mainspring of the eight impressionist exhibitions between 1874 and 1886, the figure of Sisley was more discreet. Success eluded Sisley all his life, and constant material difficulties forced him to live almost permanently in the country, far from Paris. Over thirty-five of his paintings at the Musée d'Orsay, dominated by the two masterpieces of *L'Inondation à Pont-Marly* from the Camondo bequest, show all the sites that this artist loved : Bougival, Louveciennes, Marly-le-Roi, Saint-Mammès or Moret-sur-Loing. Although less attracted than his colleagues by landscapes and the open air, Degas was an assiduous habitué of racecourses and a passionate interest in horses is reflected in both his painting and his sculpture. By virtue of the Caillebotte donation (*L'Étoile*, plus several matching pastels), the Musée d'Orsay possesses an exceptional Degas collection. The world of the opera, a major pole of attraction for this painter, is also copiously represented by his series of orchestra musicians, dance classes, ballet rehearsals and many pastels of dancers at work. In addition, there is an impressive gallery of Degas portraits (*Madame Jeantaud*, among others); the masterpiece *L'Absinthe*, which figured in the third impressionist exhibition; and a consecutive series of pastels of women at their toilette (*Le Tub*). All of these pastels show the inexhaustible technical inventiveness of Degas in the observation of "the human animal attending to its needs".

The American painter Mary Cassatt conceived a fervent admiration for Degas as soon as she saw his work at the 1874 Salon. However, she waited until 1879 before joining an impressionist exhibition, and subsequently participated in the shows of 1880, 1881, and 1886, when she presented her charming *Woman sewing*. Among the other women impressionists at the Musée d'Orsay, Berthe Morisot is best represented with her *Berceau* and the delicate *Chasse aux papillons*, whilst a single canvas testifies to the work of Eva Gonzalès, the pupil of Manet.

From 1896 onwards, the national collections were remarkably enriched with works by Renoir, thanks to the Caillebotte bequest which included *Le Moulin de la galette*, *La Balançoire* and *La Liseuse*. Today, these three paintings are among the Musée d'Orsay's greatest treasures. With more than fifty canvases, the Orsay collection gives an idea of the sheer fecundity of an artist who, like Monet, lived to a great age. Many portraits (of Bazille, Monet, Mme Alphonse Daudet, Mme Georges Charpentier, Wagner and Gabrielle, the painter's servant girl) prove Renoir's constant interest in the human face. Three paintings done in Algeria in 1881 show a new direction in the artist's style, following the frankly impressionist *Chemin dans les hautes herbes* and *Pont de chemin de fer à Chatou*. The two recently acquired *Danses* (one of which came to Orsay as a dation, the other by purchase), along with *Les Jeunes Filles au piano*, several nudes and portraits and the *Baigneuses* (given by Renoir's sons after his death), are an incomparable demonstration of the last developments in Renoir's style. Although he became an invalid at the end of his life, it is clear that he never lost one iota of his exuberant sensuality.

Monet's career, which, like Renoir's, continued well into the 20th century, to some extent followed the various subjects he painted on his travels or around his different residences. The Orsay collection of nearly seventy paintings admirably represents every period of Monet's working life. The ten pictures from the Moreau-Nélaton donation show his beginnings, followed by the Argenteuil period. The Camondo bequest (fourteen paintings) includes the Vétheuil canvases, one from London and two from Giverny that show the famous Japanese bridge (*Harmonie verte*, *Harmonie rose*) and four versions of the *Cathédrale de Rouen*, one of which had already been acquired in 1907. A more recent dation has strengthened the representation of the Giverny period with the addition of a highly coloured canvas of *Le Jardin de Monet*, and the 1981 acquisition of the *Nymphéas bleus* testifies to the development of the painter right up to his final stages, which were so rich in lessons for the painters of the 20th century.

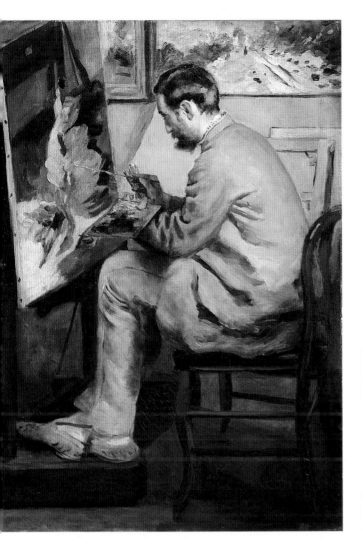

Pierre-Auguste Renoir (1841-1919)
Frédéric Bazille à son chevalet, 1867
Second impressionist exhibition, 1876
105 × 73
Bequest of Marc Bazille, brother of the model, 1924

Henri Fantin-Latour (1836-1904)
Un atelier aux Batignolles, 1870 Salon
204 × 273
Acquired in 1892

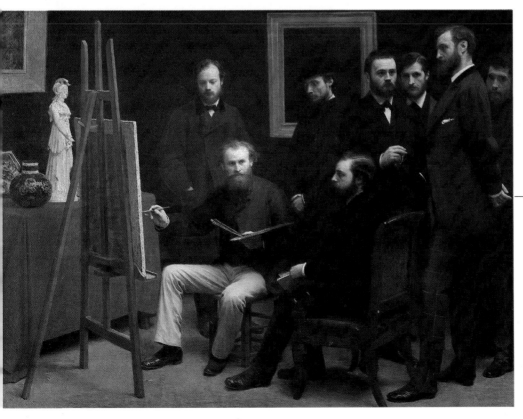

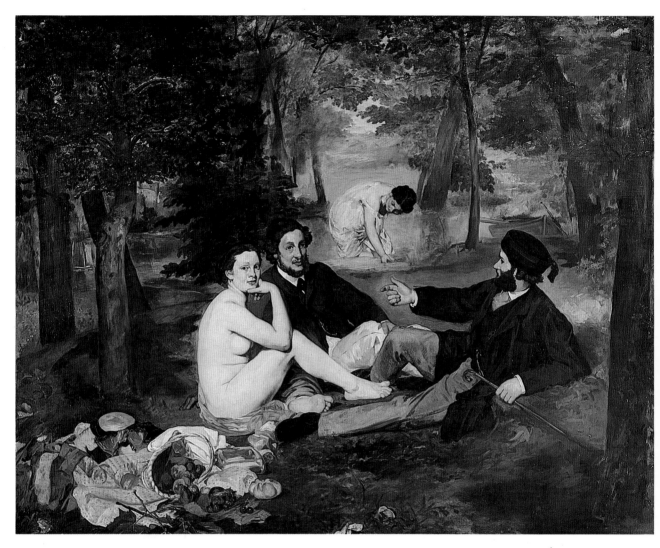

Édouard Manet (1832-1883)
Le Déjeuner sur l'herbe
Salon des refusés, 1863
208 × 264
Gift of Etienne Moreau-Nélaton, 1906

Edouard Manet (1832-1883)
Olympia, 1863. 1865 Salon
130 × 190
Acquired for the State by public subscription
on the initiative of Claude Monet, 1890

Emile Zola defended *Olympia* in the name of pure art. In 1867, in a rhetorical address to the painter, he wrote : "Tell them, *cher maître...* that for you a painting is merely a pretext for analysis. You needed a naked woman, and Olympia was the first to mind ; you needed clear, luminous patches, so you painted a bunch of flowers ; you needed something black, so you put a negress and a cat in one corner. What does it all mean ? You scarcely know, and neither do I. But I do know that you have done the work of a painter, even a great painter ; by which I mean that in your own special language you have vigorously interpreted the truths of light and shadow and the realities of objects and living creatures."

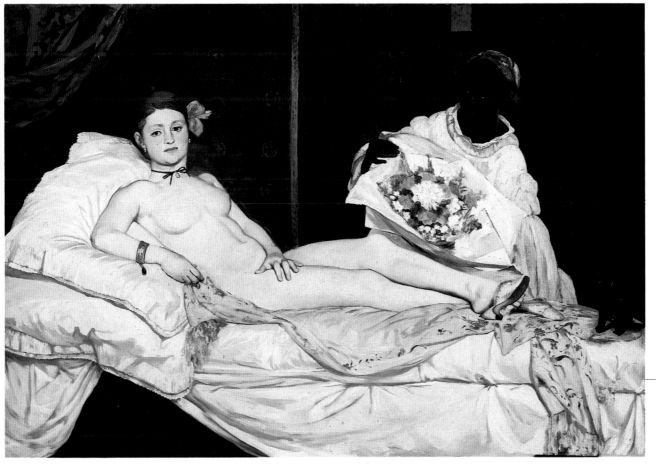

Bazille and Monet worked together constantly during the 1860s, and while their work expresses their different temperaments, it has undeniable similarities. The year he painted his own *Réunion de famille*, Bazille bought *Femme au jardin* from his friend Monet who had been rejected by the official Salon and could find no buyer for the painting. After Bazille's premature death, his father discovered that Manet possessed a portrait of Bazille by Renoir (now in the Musée d'Orsay) and offered to exchange it for *Femme au jardin*. Then, after a quarrel, Manet returned the painting to Monet, who ultimately had the satisfaction of selling it to the Musées nationaux in 1921 for a very high price.

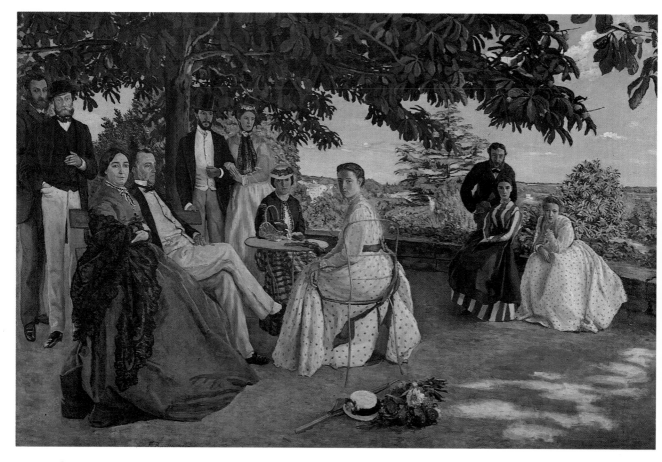

Frédéric Bazille (1841-1870)
Réunion de famille, 1867. 1868 Salon
152 × 230
Acquired with the participation of Marc Bazille
the artist's brother, 1905

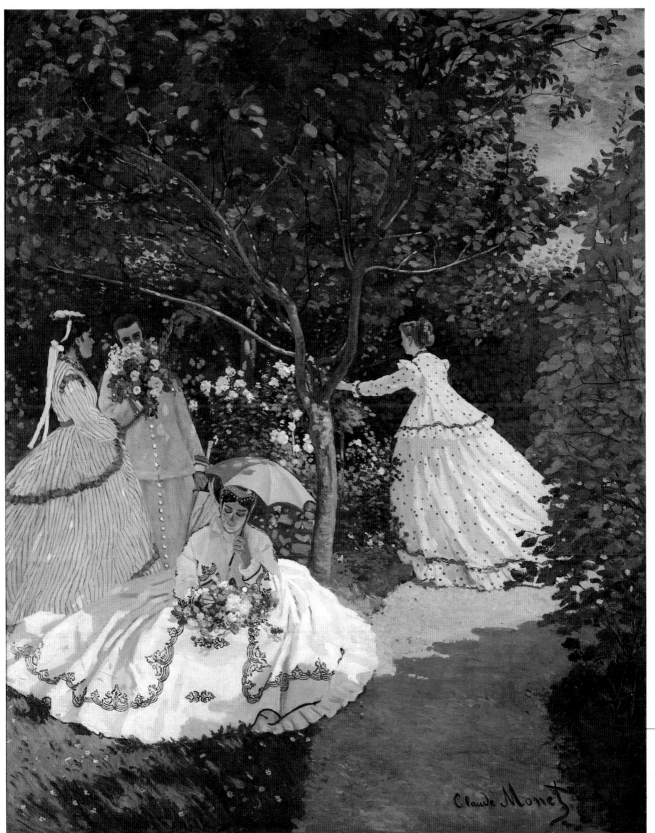

61

Claude Monet (1840-1926)
Femmes au jardin, 1866-1867
255 × 205
Acquired in 1921

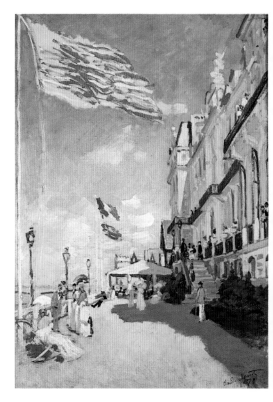

Claude Monet (1840-1926)
Hôtel des Roches Noires. Trouville, 1870
81 × 58
Gift of Jacques Laroche, subject to usufruct, 1947
admitted in 1976

Claude Monet (1840-1926)
La Pie, circa 1868-1869
89 × 130
Acquired in 1984

62

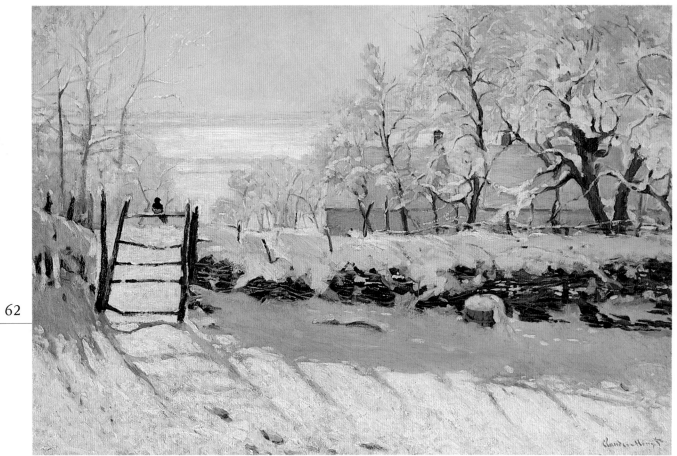

Claude Monet (1840-1926)
Déjeuner sur l'herbe, 1865-1866
248 × 217
Acquired by dation in 1987

In this ambitious painting of the *Déjeuner sur l'herbe*, started in May 1865 and left incomplete, the young 25-year-old Monet wanted to rival the great historical compositions by treating on a monumental scale a scene drawn from contemporary life.

Of the initial composition — evident in a sketch in the Pushkin Museum in Moscow — all that remains is the left part and, in particular, the central part which Monet kept in his studio until his death. These are now reunited at the Musée d'Orsay.

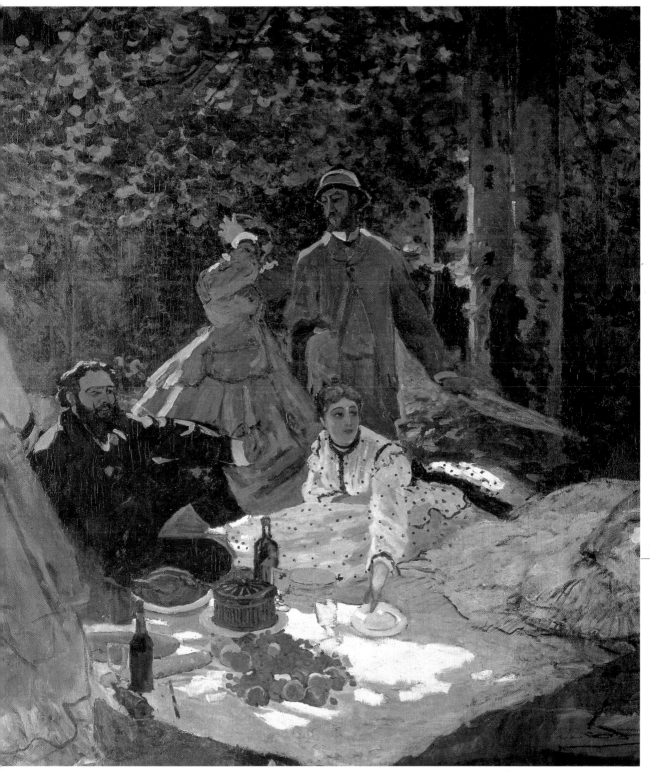

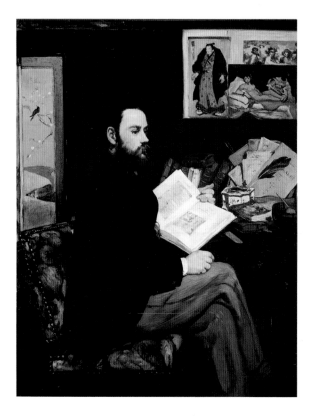

Édouard Manet (1832-1883)
Émile Zola, 1867-1868
1868 Salon
146 × 140
Gift of Mme Émile Zola
subject to usufruct, 1918
admitted in 1925

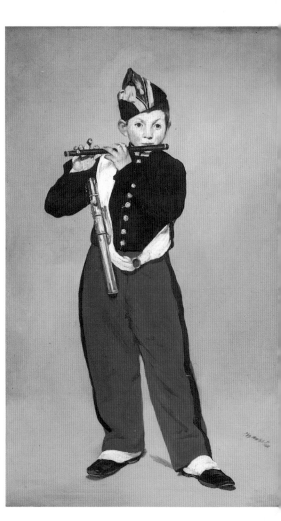

Édouard Manet (1832-1883)
Le Fifre, 1866
161 × 97
Bequest of Isaac de Camondo, 1911

Édouard Manet (1832-1883)
Sur la plage, 1873
59 × 73
Gift of
Jean-Édouard Dubrugeaud
Subject to usufruct, 1953 ;
admitted in 1970

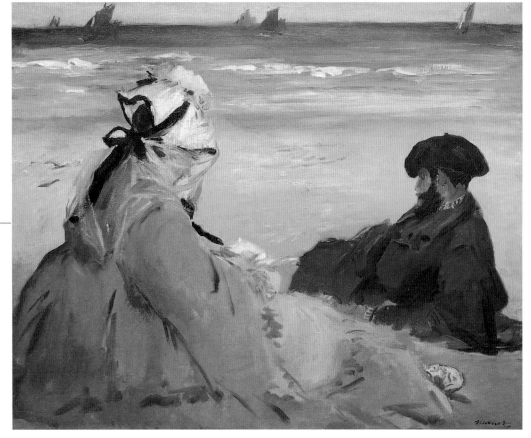

64

Édouard Manet (1832-1883)
Le Balcon, 1868-1869.
1869 Salon
170 × 124
Bequest of
Gustave Caillebotte, 1894

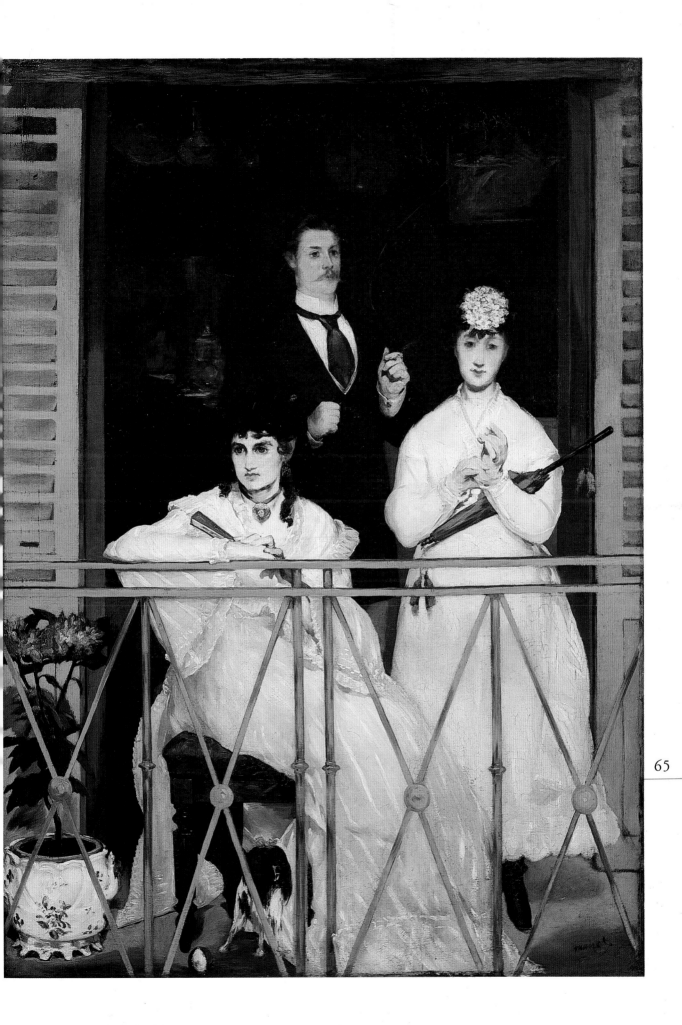

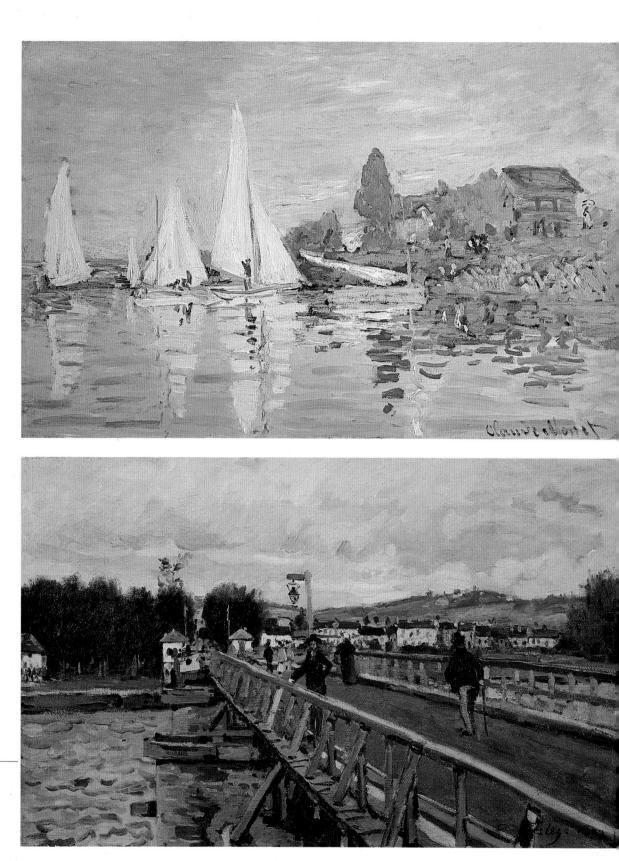

Alfred Sisley (1839-1899)
Passerelle d'Argenteuil, 1872
39 × 60
Gift of Etienne Moreau-Nélaton, 1906

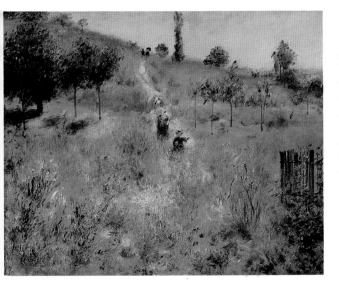

Monet came to Argenteuil at the end of 1871 to escape high Paris rents and seek out new subjects for his work. Once installed, he painted the green banks of the Seine and the sailing regattas up and down the river, which were a favourite theme since they gave him the opportunity to analyse colours reflected on water. He invited his friends to join him, with the result that Renoir, Sisley, Pissarro and even Manet all came to paint at Argenteuil, making it a symbol of the flowering of impressionism. During this period between 1872 and 1874, the movement achieved its highest degree of unity.

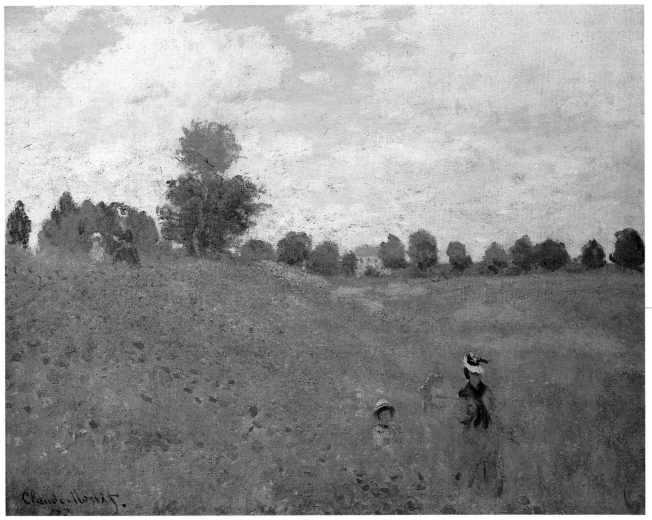

When Cézanne moved to Auvers-sur-Oise, in 1872, he found himself in close proximity to his friend at Pontoise. Although at that time Pissarro seemed to exercise a preponderant influence on Cézanne, notably by encouraging him to lighten his range of colours, there is no doubt that the latter had a reciprocal effect on Pissarro's work. Pissarro contributed to the first impressionist exhibition in 1874 (*Gelée blanche* was shown on this occasion, provoking much irony and incomprehension), and invited Cézanne to participate; this led to the first appearance of *La Maison du pendu*, a scene painted near Auvers-sur-Oise.

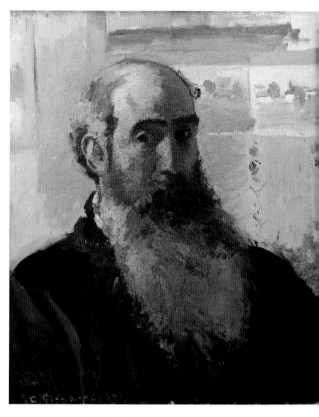

Camille Pissarro (1830-1903)
Portrait de l'artiste, 1873
56 × 46,5
Gift of Paul-Émile Pissarro, the artist's son
subject to usufruct, 1930. Admitted 1947

Camille Pissarro (1830-1903)
Gelée blanche 1873
First impressionist exhibition, 1874
65 × 93
Gift of Enriqueta Alsop
in the name of Dr Eduardo Mollard, 1972

68

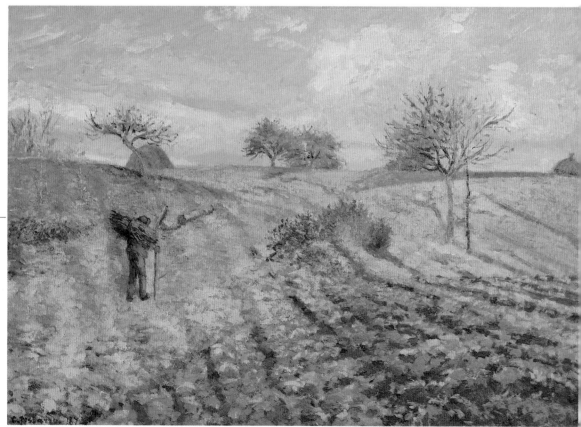

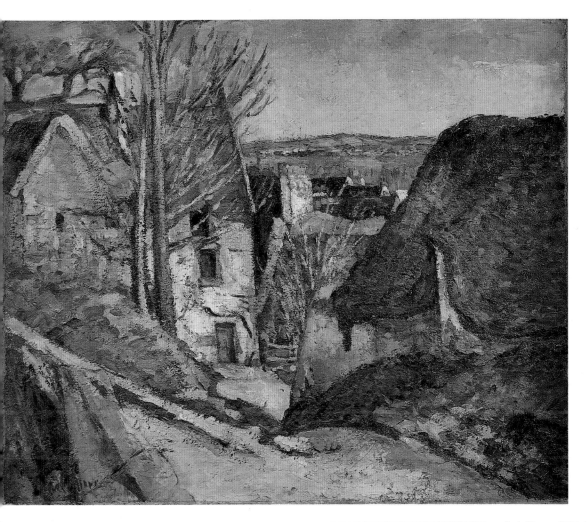

Paul Cézanne (1839-1906)
La Maison du pendu
Auvers-sur-Oise, 1873
First impressionist exhibition, 1874
55 × 66
Bequest of Isaac de Camondo, 1911

69

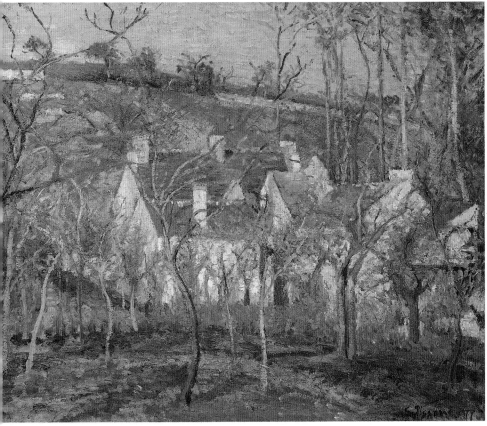

Camille Pissarro (1830-1903)
Les Toits rouges, 1877
54 × 65
Bequest of Gustave Caillebotte
1894

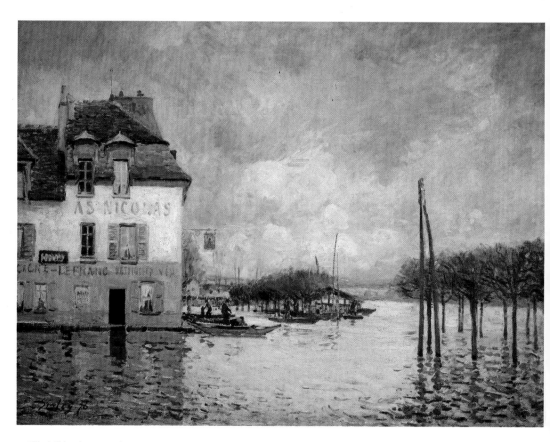

Alfred Sisley (1839-1899)
L'Inondation à Port-Marly, 1876
Shown at the second or third
impressionist exhibition, 1876 or 1877
60 × 81
Bequest of Isaac de Camondo, 1911

70

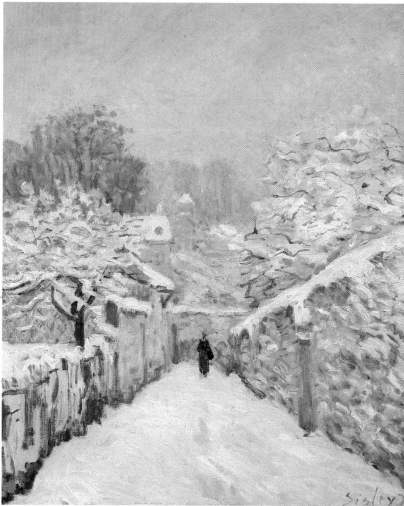

Alfred Sisley (1839-1899)
La Neige à Louveciennes, 1878
61 × 50
Bequest of Isaac de Camondo, 1911

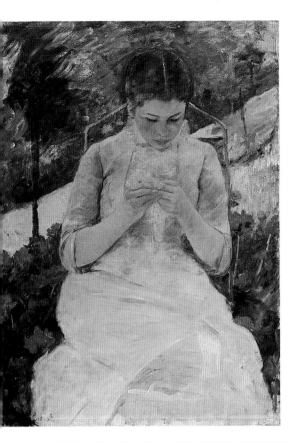

Berthe Morisot's style was essentially derived from that of Manet, with subtleties of texture which were perfectly matched to the subjects she handled. With characteristic courage, this young woman from the *haute bourgeoisie* participated in all the impressionist events (in 1874, she unveiled *Le Berceau*, a portrait of her sister Edma), except for the 1879 exhibition. Oddly enough, 1879 was the year that another woman took part for the first time : Mary Cassatt, from Pittsburgh, USA, had come to live in France not long before, and had found a mentor in Degas. The principal subjects of her paintings are women and children.

Mary Cassatt (1844-1926)
Femme cousant, circa 1880-1882
Shown at the eighth impressionist exhibition, 1886
92 × 63
Bequest of Antonin Personnaz, 1937

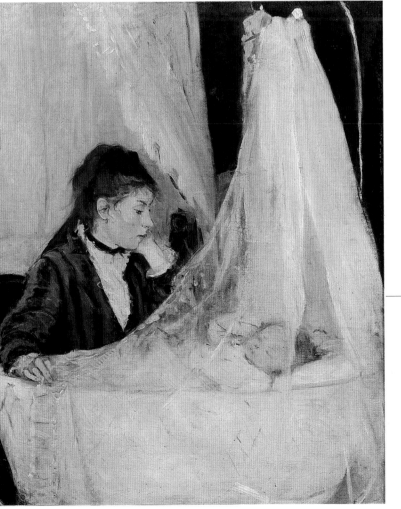

Berthe Morisot (1841-1895)
Le Berceau, 1872
Shown at the first impressionist exhibition, 1874
56 × 46
Acquired in 1930

L' *Etude; torse effet de soleil*, which reminded one hostile critic of "a pile of decomposing flesh", shows, by the iridescence of its blue-shadowed carnations, how far Renoir was able to push the study of colour. All the same, *Le Bal du moulin de la Galette* and *La Balançoire* of 1876, which depict the working class quarter of Montmartre where he lived, are probably the best examples of Renoir's impressionism. Ambitious figure composition, complex light effects, absolute freedom of touch and intensity of colour (blues that are almost black, vivid greens and oranges), are the main features of these two masterpieces, which were so ill-received by Renoir's contemporaries.

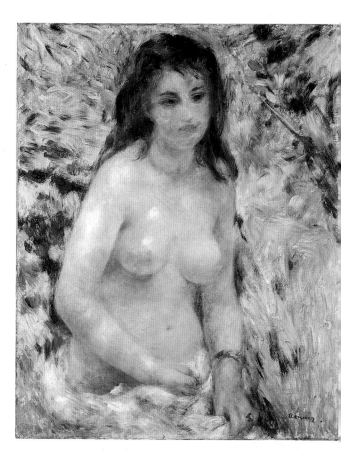

Pierre-Auguste Renoir (1841-1919)
Etude; torse, effet de soleil, 1875
Shown at the second impressionist exhibition, 1876
81 × 64
Bequest of Gustave Caillebotte, 1894

Pierre-Auguste Renoir (1841-1919)
Bal du moulin de la Galette, 1876
Shown at the third impressionist exhibition, 1877
131 × 175
Bequest of Gustave Caillebotte, 1894

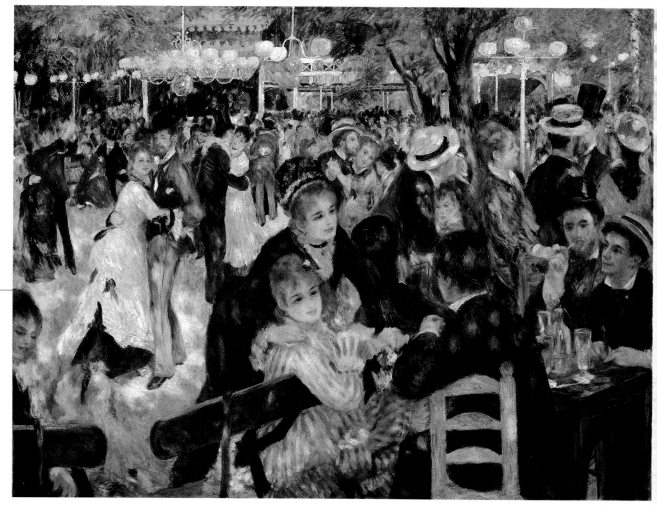

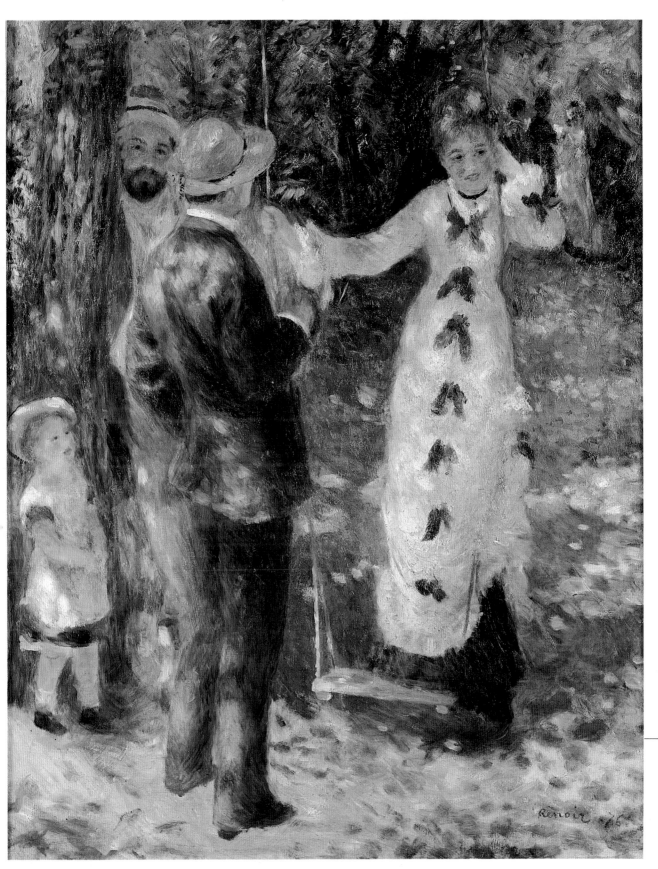

Pierre-Auguste Renoir (1841-1919)
La Balançoire, 1876
Shown at the third impressionist exhibition, 1877
92 × 73
Bequest of Gustave Caillebotte, 1894

For Monet and his colleagues, Paris in the aftermath of Haussmann's changes offered a fresh new artistic theme. It was not so much the buildings that interested Monet as the seething life of the boulevards, the foliage of the parks, and the intense colours of the flags put out on holidays; these he rendered in sensitive, delicate brushwork, in compositions that were allusive to the point of abstraction. Another modern subject, the Gare Saint-Lazare, reveals Monet's taste for repetition of the same theme in various lights: two versions of this theme have come down to us.

Claude Monet (1840-1926)
La Gare Saint-Lazarre
Shown at the third impressionist exhibition, 1877
75 × 104
Bequest of Gustave Caillebotte, 1894

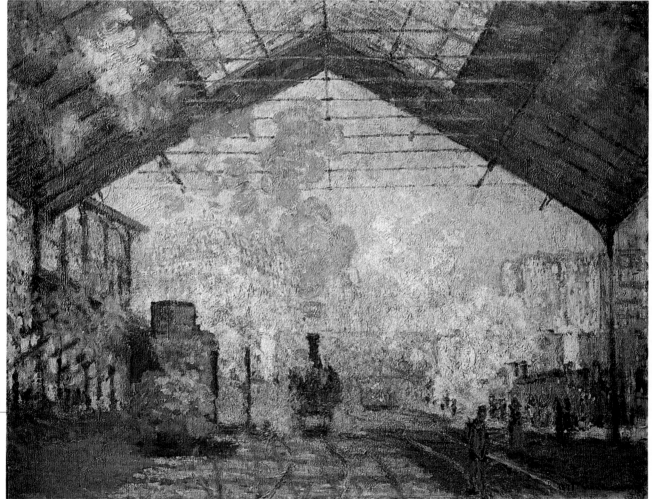

74

Claude Monet (1840-1926)
La Rue Montorgueil. Fête du 30 juin 1878, 1878
Shown at the fourth impressionist exhibition, 1879
80 × 50
Acquired by dation in 1982

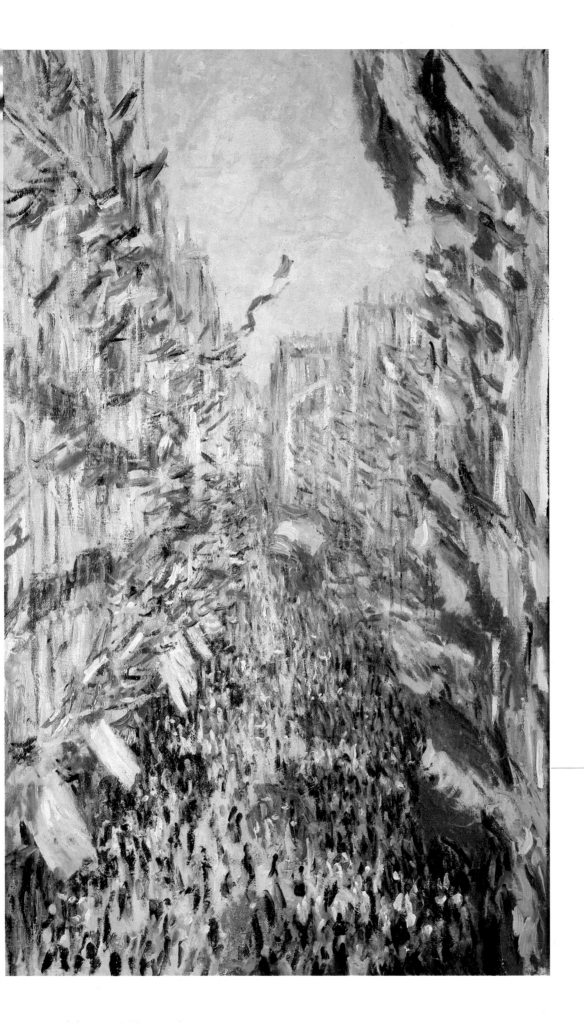

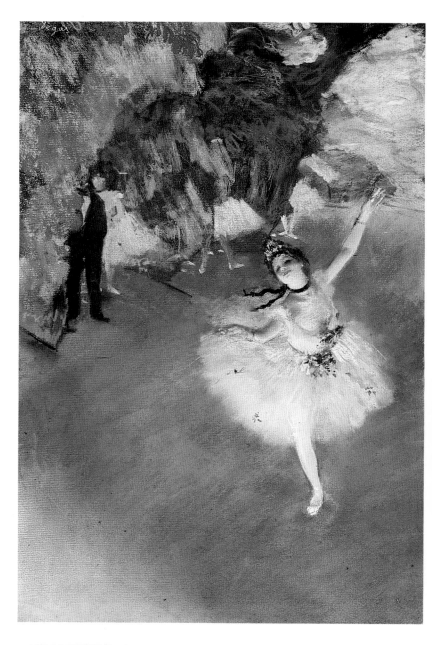

Edgar Degas (1834-1917)
L'Étoile, circa 1878
Pastel, 60 × 44
Bequest of Gustave Caillebotte, 1894

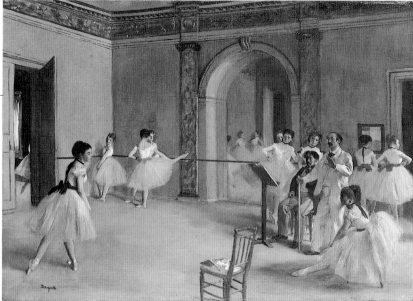

Edgar Degas (1834-1917)
*Le Foyer de la danse à l'Opéra
de la rue Le Peletier*, 1872
32 × 46
Bequest of Isaac de Camondo, 1911

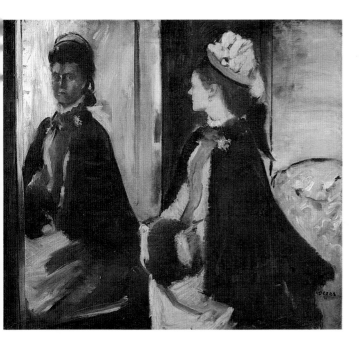

egas once proclaimed : "No art is as unspontaneous as mine. What I do is the result of contemplation and the study of the old masters." This may be surprising, in view of the fact that most of Degas' paintings seem to express an immediate ephemeral reality. His attention to human nature and enthusiasm for detail shine through in nearly every case. Moreover, Degas' care and sensitivity for line has the effect of defining clear forms within subtly constructed or suggested spaces—see the play of reflections in *Madame Jeantaud* or the apparently suspended composition of the tables in *L'Absinthe*.

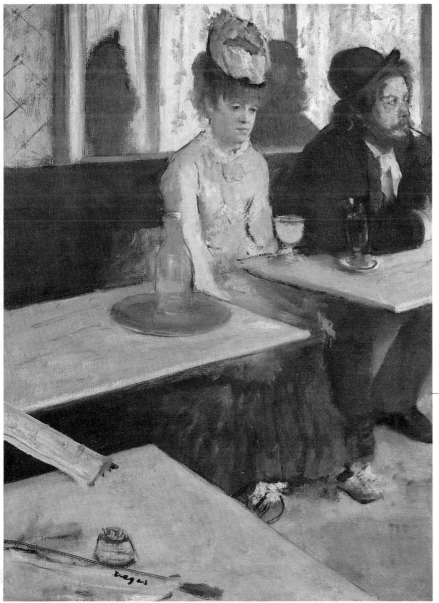

Edgar Degas (1834-1917)
Madame Jeantaud au miroir, circa 1875
70 × 84
Bequest of Jean-Edouard Dubrujeaud
subject to usufruct for his son
Jean Angladon-Dubrujeaud, 1970
usufruct ceded, 1970

77

Edgar Degas (1834-1917)
Au café or *l'Absinthe*, 1876
92 × 68
Gift of Isaac de Camondo, 1911

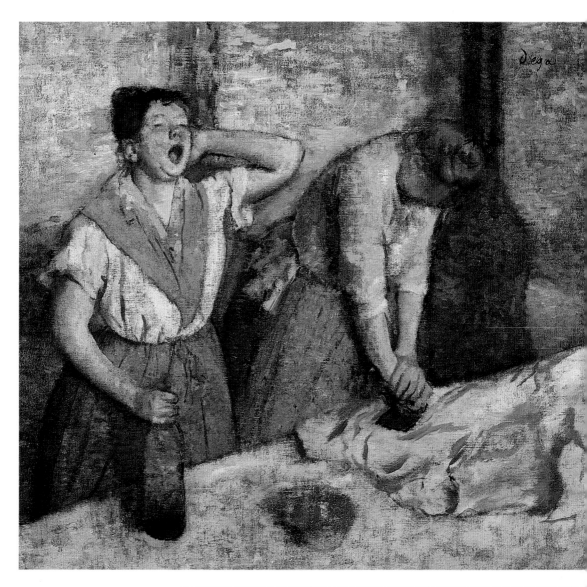

Edgar Degas (1834-1917)
Les Repasseuses, circa 1884
76 × 81
Bequest of Isaac de Camondo, 1911

78

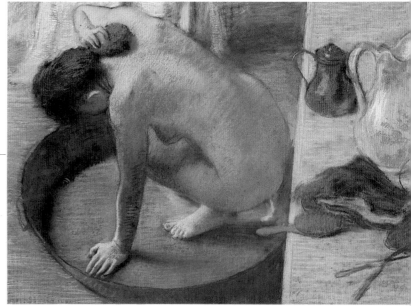

Edgar Degas (1834-1917)
Le Tub, 1886
Pastel, 60 × 83
Bequest of Isaac de Camondo, 1911

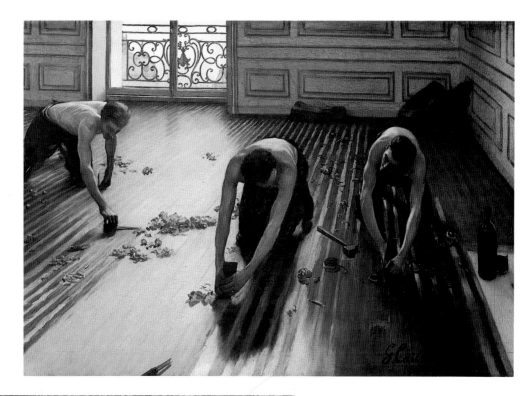

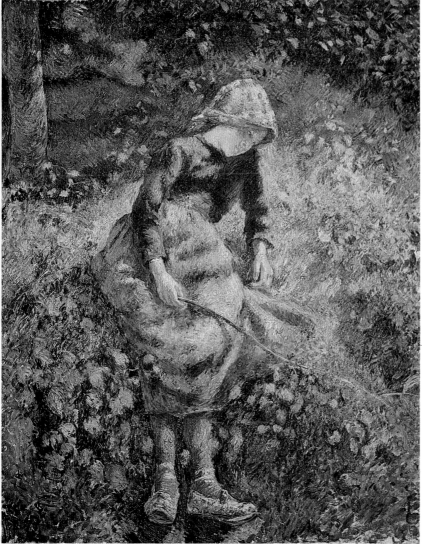

Gustave Caillebotte (1848-1894)
Les Raboteurs de parquet, 1875
Shown at the second impressionist exhibition, 1876
192 × 146
Gift of the heirs of Gustave Caillebotte, 1894

Camille Pissarro (1830-1903)
Jeune fille à la baguette, 1881
Shown at the seventh impressionist exhibition, 1882
81 × 64
Bequest of Isaac de Camondo, 1911

Pierre-Auguste Renoir (1841-1919)
Danse à la ville, 1883
180 × 90
Acquired by dation 1978

Pierre-Auguste Renoir (1841-1919)
Danse à la campagne, 1883
180 × 90
Acquired in 1970

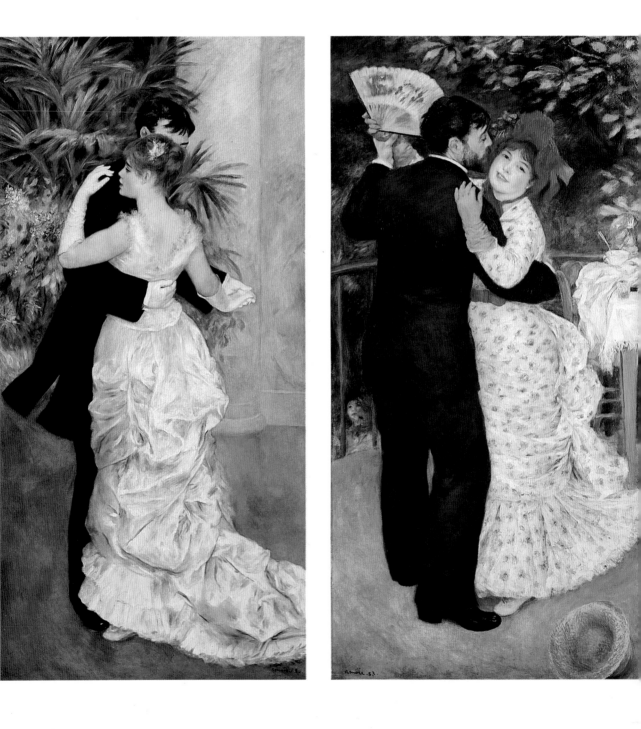

80

Less than ten years separate *Le Bal du moulin de la Galette* and Renoir's *Danses*. The similarity of the two themes accentuates the speed of Renoir's development, as well as the completeness of his rupture in 1880 with the vague contours, complex treatment of space and shimmering colours of his impressionist period. Curiously, the model for *Danse à la ville* was Suzanne Valadon, the mother of Utrillo ; the dancer in the other canvas was Aline Charigot, later Mme Renoir. Painted nearly forty years later, *Les Baigneuses*, the artist's final masterpiece, testifies to his ultimate experiment with form, space and colour.

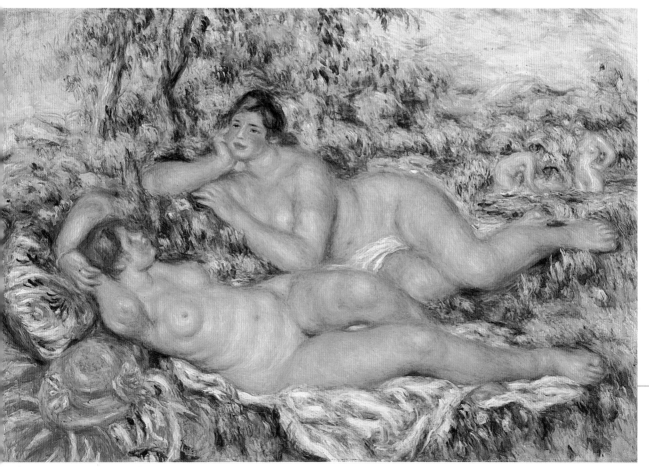

81

Pierre-Auguste Renoir (1841-1919)
Baigneuses, 1919
110 × 160
Gift of the artist's sons, 1983

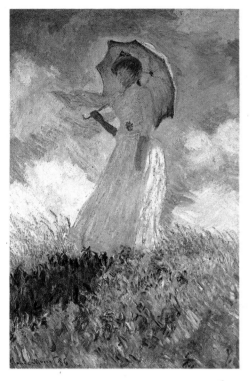

As Monet explained to the critic Duret, one of the most faithful allies of the impressionists, he worked ''on figures in the open air... treated in the same way as landscapes''. The two *Femmes à l'ombrelle* show how Monet's themes, his human figures, his façades of Rouen cathedral or even his pond at Giverny were used merely as a pretext to display the realities of colour and light as he perceived them.

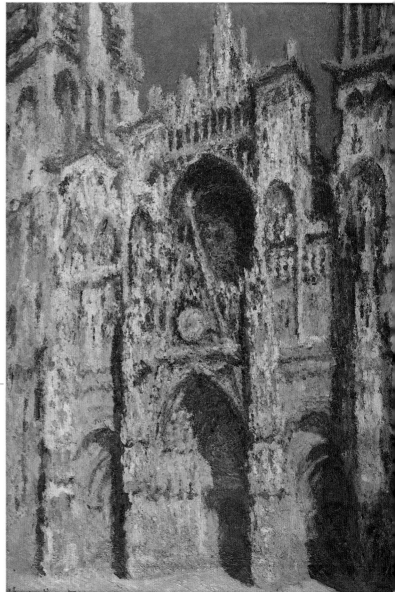

82

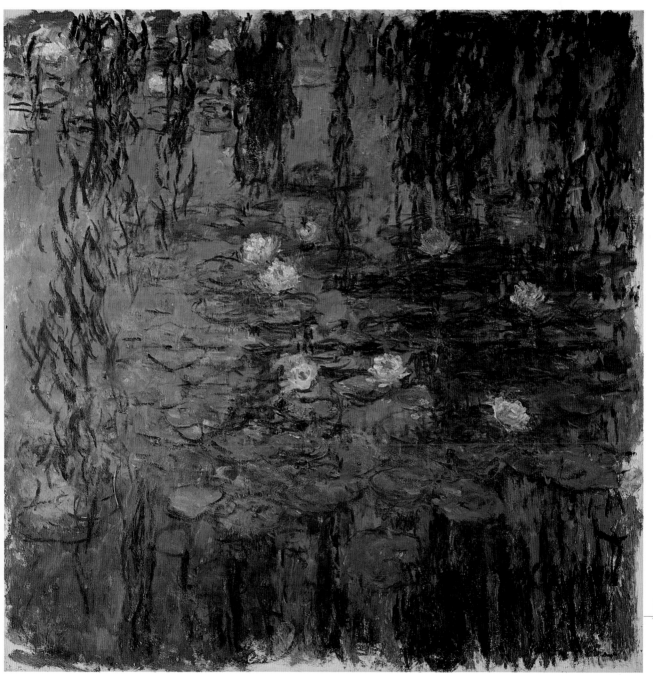

Claude Monet (1840-1926)
Nymphéas bleus, after 1917
200 × 200
Acquired in 1981

84

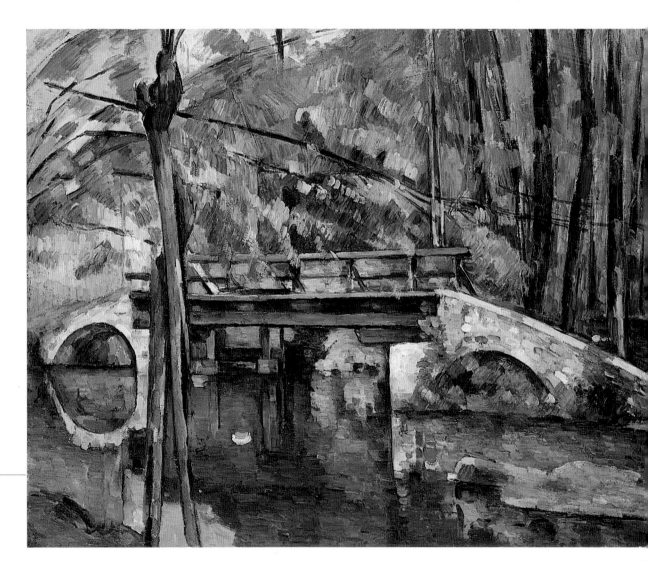

Paul Cézanne (1839-1906)
Le Pont de Maincy, près de Melun, 1879-1880
58 × 72
Acquired on the arrears of an anonymous
Canadian donation, 1955

Post-impressionism

Monet, Renoir and Pissarro by no means exhausted the resources of impressionism, and already by the 1880s a series of reactions to the movement had begun, headed by different painters. Some, like Cézanne, had been associated with the early stages of the impressionist adventure ; others, like Gauguin, Van Gogh or Seurat, belonged to the succeeding generation, or were even younger, like Toulouse-Lautrec or the nabis. Soon enough, it became expedient to refer to the crop of new artistic tendencies as "post-impressionist" ; they were highly varied, defined themselves with reference to impressionism, and were frequently in open reaction to it. Cézanne's construction and Gauguin's syntheticism were a response to the dissolution of forms, which was the logical outcome of Monet's work. The latter's spontaneity of touch was in direct opposition to the divisionist rationalism of Seurat and the neo-impressionists. The instanteousness of the impression imprisoned in reality, was answered by Redon's leap into the inner world and the expression of his visions of fantasy, or by Van Gogh's free use of the suggestive power of colour.

About thirty of Cézanne's paintings are exhibited at the Musée d'Orsay, covering every stage of his career. This unique collection is principally derived from important bequests and donations, impressive both in quality and quantity (Caillebotte, Camondo, Pellerin, Gachet, Kaganovitch). To these have been added other works acquired in 1978 by dation (*Rochers près de Château noir*, from the former Matisse collection) and, in 1982, a group of twelve paintings from the Pellerin collection, five of which were assigned to the museum (*La Pastorale*). It was not until 1949 that a smaller version of the *Baigneurs* of 1890-1900 was purchased, together with one of the artist's first works, *La Madeleine* (circa 1868-1869), a fragment from the decoration of Jas-de-Bouffan, Cézanne's father's property at Aix.

We owe the first Cézannes in the national collections to Caillebotte. These were *La Cour de ferme à Auvers* and the lovely *Estanquet*, the site of a property owned by Cézanne's mother. This landscape, built up brushstroke by brushstroke and immortalised in a light that suspends all movement, has nothing in common with the seascapes done by the artist's impressionist colleagues. *Le Pont de Maincy*, which was painted during the same period and deals with a favourite impressionist theme, shows how Cézanne distanced himself from a style which did not satisfy his own deeper preoccupations, namely the primacy of spatial organisation, the construction of forms by brushstroke, and the obstinate will to transcend the temporal contingencies inherent in the subject. These elements are not yet visible in the seven paintings donated by Paul Gachet between 1951 and 1954 ; all of these were completed around 1873, a period that was heavily influenced by Pissarro (notably *La Maison du docteur Gachet* or *Carrefour de la rue Rémy à Auvers*). Apart from the *Portrait of Achille Emperaire* in the former Pellerin collection, the Musée d'Orsay possesses two more historic canvases which represented Cézanne's work at the first impressionist exhibition in 1874 : *Une moderne Olympia* from the Gachet donation and *La Maison du pendu* from the fabulous Camondo bequest of 1911. The Camondo bequest also included the famous *Vase bleu*, one of the five versions of *Joueurs de cartes* and the impressive *Nature morte, pommes et oranges* (1890). The latter, with the three still lifes from the Pellerin bequest and *La Femme à la cafetière* constitute a unique ensemble which allows us to follow the painter's development from 1877 to his maturity in the 1890s.

The art of Van Gogh also began in juxtaposition with impressionism, during his stay in Paris between February 1886 and February 1888; his discovery of the movement led to the blossoming of his own art, which at the Musée d'Orsay is represented by no less than twenty canvases. *La Tête de paysanne hollandaise* painted in 1884, is the sole example in the collection of Van Gogh's earlier work; this period with its dark, heavily-applied paint was dominated by the famous *Mangeurs de pommes de terre*, for which *La Tête de paysanne* was a preliminary sketch. The latter painting is also the only Van Gogh actually purchased by the Musées nationaux (1954). Apart from the State's participation in the acquisition of *L'Église d'Auvers*, all the Van Goghs in the collection derive from various gifts and bequests, notably the two separate Gachet donations.

Van Gogh's Paris period is illustrated by five paintings at the Musée d'Orsay. It was at this time that the painter, who had come to Paris to join his brother Theo, found himself swept up in an artistic milieu that was literally seething with excitement and new ideas. The immediate effect was an irreversible lightening of Van Gogh's palette, then dominated by dark ochres and sepia browns as in *La Guinguette* and *Le Restaurant de la sirène*, which were frankly impressionist. But Van Gogh's impetuous temperament had only needed an adequate technique by which to express itself: soon he was discovering the expressive power of pure colour applied in separate touches and juxtaposed, as in *Fritillaires*, the *Self-Portrait* of 1887, and the famous *Italienne*. The composition of this last painting, which anticipates the boldness of the fauvists and the expressionists, betrays the decisive influence of Japanese prints, which the artist had recently discovered.

From Van Gogh's stay in Arles, the museum possesses four pictures, of which *L'Arlésienne* and *La Salle de danse* show Gauguin's powerful influence. The 1889 *Self-Portrait*, *La Chambre à Arles* and *La Méridienne* are suffused with a special emotional intensity, because these three canvases were done in the Hôpital Saint-Jean at Saint-Rémy, to which the artist had voluntarily committed himself. Finally, seven paintings from the Gachet donation (among them the famous *Église d'Auvers* and *Portrait du docteur Gachet*) show Van Gogh's final pre-fauvist and expressionist phase in his last years at Auvers-sur-Oise.

A revival of interest in the neo-impressionist school, which for years was ill-represented in the national collections, came somewhat too late to fill various lacunae in the museums. Indeed, most of the masterpieces painted by the movement's principal exponent, Georges Seurat, were sold abroad during the 1920s; although Signac's request to the American collector John Quinn did result in the return of Seurat's last painting in 1924. This was *Le Cirque*, left unfinished at Seurat's death in 1891. Apart from this, the Musée d'Orsay has to make do with three interesting studies, or *croquetons* for the master's two great works, *La Baignade à Asnières* and *Un dimanche après-midi à l'île de la Grande Jatte*. Fortunately, the additional purchase of three detailed studies for *Les Poseuses* and *Port-en-Bessin* in 1952 enable us to gain a fair idea of the art of Seurat in his maturity.

It is also a matter for regret that some of Signac's most important paintings were not acquired in time to prevent their loss abroad. Nonetheless, his work is abundantly represented at the Musée d'Orsay, from the impressionist landscape of *La Route de Gennevilliers* (1883) to the imposing *Port de La Rochelle* (1921) with its broad, square brushwork, and the strict divisionism of *La Seine à Herblat* (1889), *Les Provençales au puits* and the striking *Bouée rouge* (1895).

A donation by Ginette Signac in 1976 has considerably enriched the State collection of neo-impressionists, with (among other works) two paintings by Signac and two by Henri-Edmond Cross, including *L'Air du soir* (1894). Cross is better represented than his fellows due to a series of important purchases of his work between 1947 and 1969 : *Les Iles d'or*, *Le Portrait de Mme Cross* and *La Chevelure* were acquired during this period and together are highly representative of the artist's subtle pointillist technique in the years 1891-1892.

Les Batteurs de pieux and *Une rue de Paris sous la Commune* illustrate the realism of M. Luce, along with his portraits of his friend Cross and of the critic Félix Fénéon. Angrand, Dubois-Pillet, Lucien Pissarro and Petitjean are also present at the Musée d'Orsay, while a few paintings by Théo Van Rysselberghe and one by G. Lemmen show the Belgian continuation of neo-impressionism.

With its collection of eighteen oils on canvas or *à l'essence sur carton* (turpentine on hardboard), the Musée d'Orsay offers a rich overview of the work of Toulouse-Lautrec (to which the astonishing museum at Albi is exclusively devoted). Apart from the two fine panels done for la Goulue's booth at the Foire du trône (1895), the Orsay collection consists of average-size works, most of which are portraits. From pure portraiture (*Justine Dieuhl*) to rapid sketches of servant girls and toilet scenes in the tradition of Degas, the various aspects of Toulouse-Lautrec are well represented, especially his theatre characters, with *La Goulue*, *Valentin le Désossé*, *Cha-u-kao*, *Jane Avril* and *Henry Samary*. *Seule*, which came recently to the museum by dation, demonstrates the artist's technical virtuosity in the service of unvarnished realism ; as well as his poignant vision, echoing the extraordinary series of 1895 lithographs entitled *Elles*.

All these works except three came from bequests or donations made between 1902 and 1953 ; notably the Personnaz bequest of four paintings, which included *Jane Avril* and *Le Lit*.

Odile Redon was a major figure of the post-impressionist generation, whose painted work has been neglected by State museums for many years. Till recently, the national collection contained only six paintings by him : the posthumous *Portrait of Gauguin*, the *Portrait of Mme Redon*, *les Yeux clos* (the only painting bought by the State from the artist during his lifetime, in 1904), *Eve*, recently acquired by dation, and two bouquets of flowers. The museum's selection of Redon's pastels, which include masterpieces such as *Parsifal*, *Le Sacré-Cœur*, *Le Char d'Apollon* and *Bouddha* had to compensate for the lack of oils, until the 1984 bequest of Mme Suzanne Redon, which proved to be an event of major importance. Hundreds of drawings were given to the Louvre by this bequest and the Musée d'Orsay inherited about sixty pictures by Redon, among them a youthful *Self-Portrait*, a charming *Portrait d'Ari enfant*, various religious, mythological or literary scenes (*Le Sommeil de Caliban*), and a unique ensemble of landscapes. Among the pastels, *Jeanne d'Arc*, *La Couronne* and above all the famous *Coquille* display Redon's incomparable mastery of this subtle medium.

A special place in the museum is reserved for Henri Rousseau, known as the "Douanier". This marginal painter, a Paris customs service employee, is represented by the three important canvases : *La Guerre*, *Portrait de femme* and *La Charmeuse de serpents*, which demonstrate the great originality of a painter who intrigued Pissarro and Gauguin, amused Jarry and delighted Apollinaire and Picasso.

A desire for exoticism and a certain non-conformist bent were characteristics that Douanier Rousseau shared with Gauguin. The latter, having begun as a weekend impressionist heavily influenced by Pissarro, eventually fled the constraints of Paris to settle in Brittany. At Pont-Aven, between the summer of 1886 and the autumn of 1888, a completely new style was born of the confrontation between Émile Bernard, a young painter and theoretician, and Gauguin, with his exile's shyness and anguish. Together, they contrived a form of synthetic painting, breaking with traditional perspective in pictures filled with bright colours and ringed by flat tints : hence the name of "cloisonnism" given to their technique. They drew their inspiration from popular imagery and local traditions, notably pastoral scenes. The group of painters that grew up around them at Pouldu in 1889 was quickly reinforced by the arrival of new aspirants such as Laval, Sérusier, Schuffenecker, Séguin, Roy, and the Dutchman Meyer de Haan...

The museum's collection of paintings from the school of Pont-Aven is especially characteristic of the development of public taste, and of the incomprehension which dogged this school of painting until the 1950s. It was not until twenty years after his death in 1923, that Gauguin entered the Musée du Luxembourg with *Les Alyscamps* and *Femmes de Tahiti*. Four years later, *La Belle Angèle*, a canvas that is particularly representative of the Brittany period and which had belonged for a time to Degas, was donated by the dealer Ambroise Vollard with whom Gauguin had contracted during his lifetime. But it was only in the 1950s that renewed interest began to be shown in Gauguin's Breton style and the school of Pont-Aven in general. This interest ran parallel to a revival of interest in the neo-impressionists and the nabis, as if people were suddenly discovering the importance of the post-impressionist movements in the development of 20th-century painting. The recent acquisition of *Madeleine au bois d'Amour* and *La Moisson au bord de la mer* has restored Émile Bernard to his rightful place in the evolution of the new style, while Sérusier is now well-represented by virtue of the donation and bequest of Mlle Boutaric, the heiress of the artist. This bequest included seven paintings, among them *L'Ève bretonne* and *Les Laveuses*, which show the symbolist and synthesist aspect of Sérusier's work. Furthermore, the Musée d'Orsay has just purchased his famous *Talisman*, with the aid of an anonymous donor. No-one could hope for a better transition between the school of Pont-Aven and the nabi movement than this little work, whose historic importance has been stressed by Maurice Denis himself in his *Théories*.

Although the museum still lacks a painting dating from Gauguin's stay in Martinique in 1887, we can judge of his two periods in Tahiti by an ensemble of very fine works demonstrating the synthetic, decorative, highly coloured style he developed in the Tropics. These include *le Repas*, *Arearea* and *Vairumati*.

Sérusier's *Le Talisman* will enlighten the visitor as to the genesis of the nabi group in the autumn of 1888. Bonnard, Vuillard, Maurice Denis, Roussel and Ranson, who had studied together at the Académie Julian or the Ecole des Beaux-Arts, were quickly joined by the Swiss painter Vallotton, and the sculptor Maillol. As prophets of a new art—*nabi* means prophet in Hebrew—this group absorbed the lessons of Gauguin and developed the Japanese, ornamental aspect of their work, in an attempt to bypass simple easel painting in favour of a broader, more decorative approach. Recent acquisitions, especially of paintings by Bonnard (through purchases, gifts, donations and bequests) have considerably strengthened an already abundant reserve, making the Musée d'Orsay's collection one of the foremost repositories of nabi works in the world. *Le Peignoir* and *Le Corsage à carreaux* (acquired in 1939 and 1947) show the strong Japanese influence that permeates Bonnard's art, whilst the extensive Vuillard bequest of 1941 (including *Au lit*, a typical example of the nabi aesthetic), added to a reserve which already boasted the three panels of *Jardins publics* and the charming *Le Sommeil* (1891).

Maurice Denis, the theoretician of the group, is well represented by symbolist and intimist works (*Les Muses* and *La Famille Mellerio*), while a fine sequence of Vallottons shows the originality and humour of this singular artist. The whole nabi group is portrayed in Maurice Denis' *Hommage à Cézanne*, which was painted just before the various members split up and went their own artistic ways.

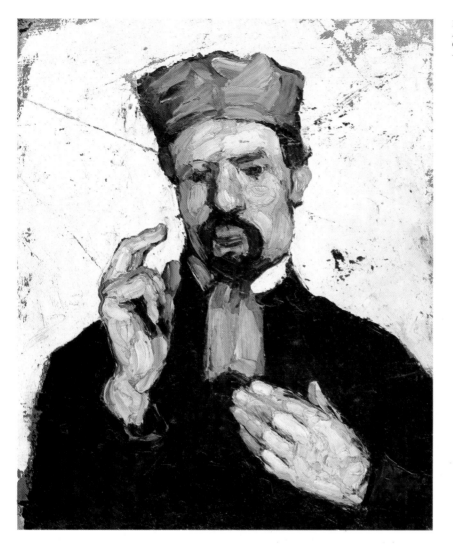

Paul Cézanne (1839-1906)
L'Avocat (Uncle Dominique), 1866
65 × 54,5
Acquired by dation in 1991

L'Avocat, which dates from the beginning of Cézanne's career, represents the artist's maternal uncle, Dominique Aubert, a familiar model who appears in dozens of portraits where he is represented in a more or less fantastic style, rendered in energetic strokes from a palette knife.
The *Pastorale* also belongs to the artist's "couillarde" style, expressing a powerful temperament preyed on by violent conflicts, translated to the canvas in thick paint and strong contrasts. Moreover, in choosing a classical theme for the *Pastorale* — a glance at Manet's *Déjeuner sur l'Herbe* — Cézanne transferred his admiration for the grand Italian baroque style and set in motion the *Baigneuses* series which obsessed him throughout his life.

90

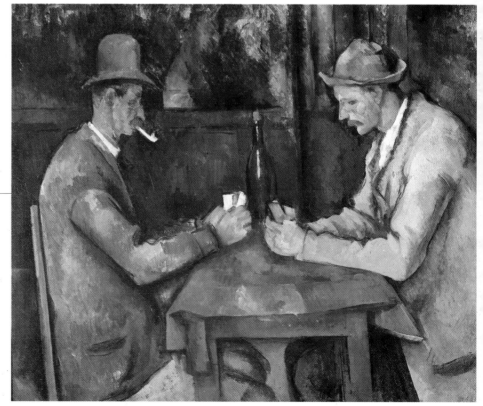

Paul Cézanne (1839-1906)
Les Joueurs de cartes, circa 1890-1895
47 × 57
Bequest of Isaac de Camondo, 1911

Paul Cézanne (1839-1906)
Baigneurs, circa 1890-1892
60 × 82
Gift of baroness Eva Gebhard-Gourgaud, 1965

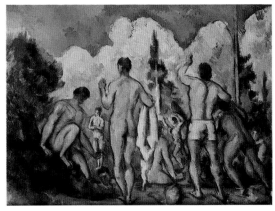

Paul Cézanne (1839-1906)
Pastorale or *Idylle*, 1870
65 × 81
Acquired by dation, 1982

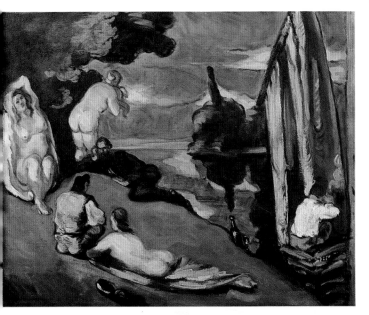

Paul Cézanne (1839-1906)
L'Estaque, seen from the gulf of Marseilles, circa 1878-1879
59 × 73
Bequest of Gustave Caillebotte, 1894

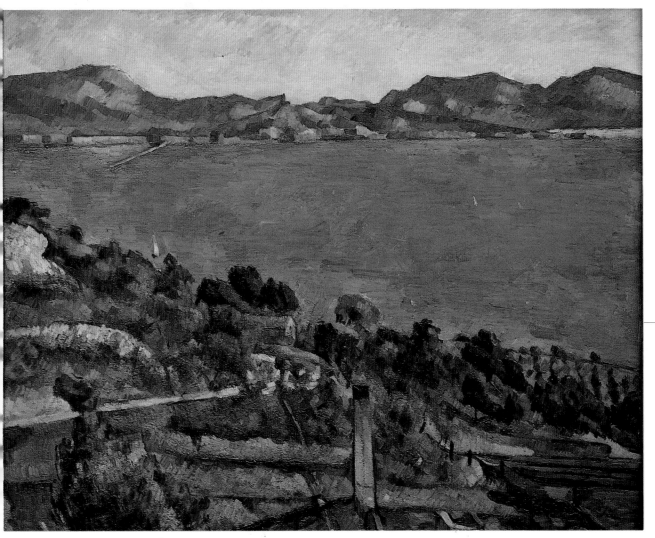

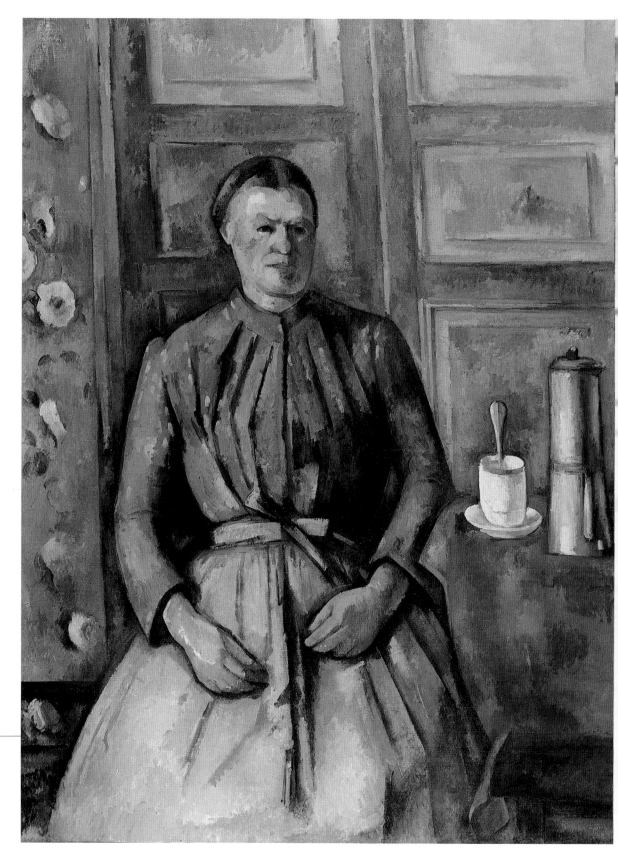

Paul Cézanne (1839-1906)
La Femme à la cafetière, circa 1890-1895
130 × 96
Gift of M. et Mme Jean-Victor Pellerin, 1956

Paul Cézanne (1839-1906)
Nature morte ; pommes et oranges, circa 1895-1900
74 × 93
Bequest of Isaac de Camondo, 1911

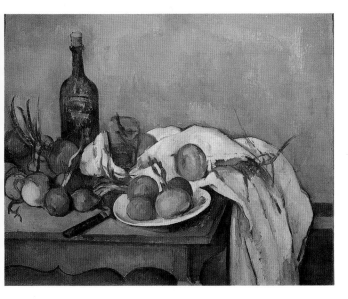

I want to astonish Paris with an apple'', said the young Cézanne, according to the famous critic, Gustave Geffroy, who was the first owner of his *Nature morte, pommes et oranges*. Cézanne's purpose in his portraits and still lifes was to situate the subject or model in space by increasing the number of angles from which it may be viewed ; to question the subject's basic structural characteristics ; then to study the incidence of light upon it, in order to endow it with the maximum sensory effect as a painting. ''When colour is at its richest, form is at its fullest'', Cézanne liked to say. By endorsing the autonomy of the painted object in this way, he opened wide the door that led to cubism and abstract art.

Paul Cézanne (1839-1906)
Nature morte aux oignons, circa 1895
66 × 82
Bequest of Auguste Pellerin, 1929

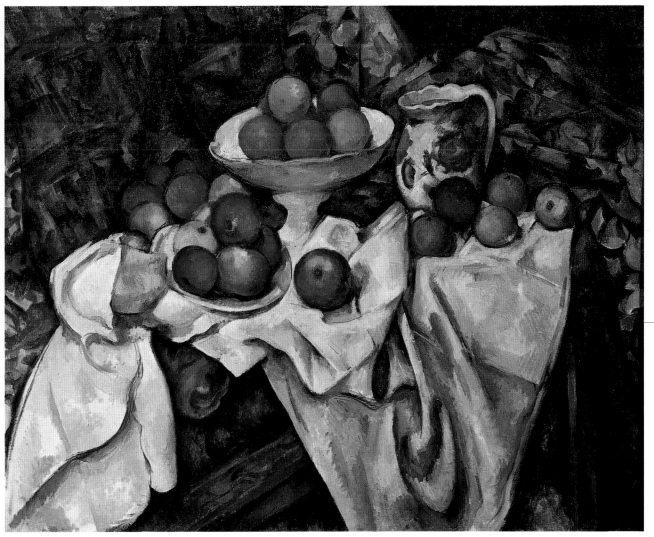

93

olour must do the work here, and it must give things greater style by simplifying them, so as to be suggestive of rest and sleep in general. Ultimately, the sight of the picture should soothe the mind, or rather the imagination.'' These words were written by Van Gogh to his brother Theo at the time that he was painting the first version of his *Chambre à Arles* in 1888. A year later, still in hospital at Saint-Rémy, he undertook two replicas of this picture, one of which is at the Musée d'Orsay today. Viewed in retrospect, this room is the focus of all Van Gogh's dreams, and its collapsing perspective is a denunciation of emptiness. Like his *Self-Portrait*, the painting shows how the sick Van Gogh pathetically used the exercise of painting as a palliative for the torments he was undergoing.

Vincent Van Gogh (1853-1890)
L'Italienne, 1887
81 × 60
Donation of baroness Eva Gebhard-Gourgaud, 1965

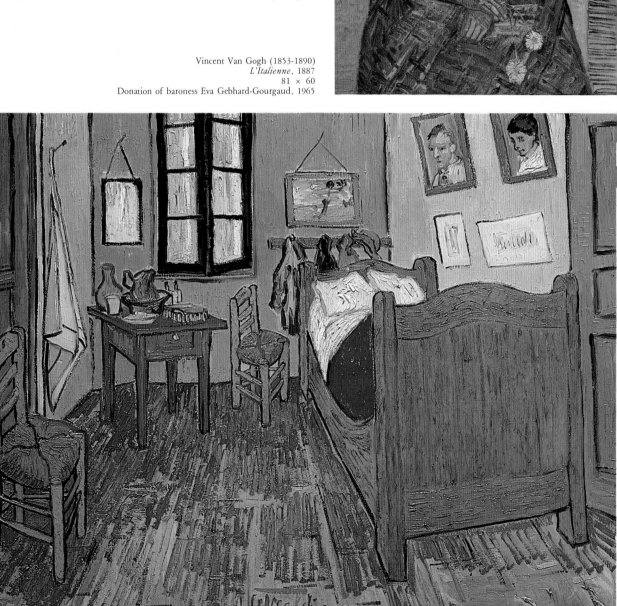

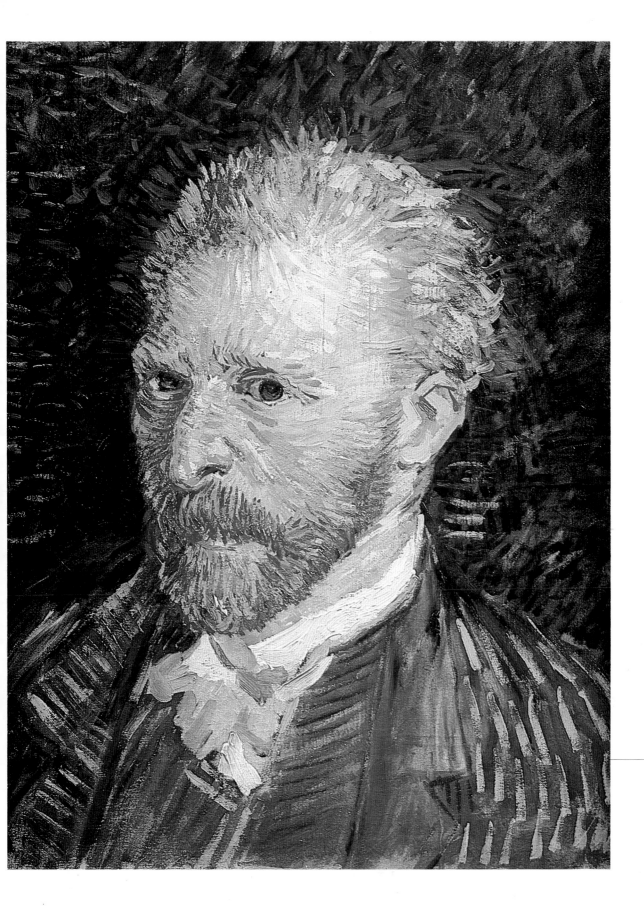

Vincent Van Gogh (1853-1890)
La Chambre de Van Gogh à Arles, 1889
57 × 74
From the former Matsukata collection ; admitted in 1959
in application of the peace treaty with Japan

Vincent Van Gogh (1853-1890)
Portrait de l'artiste, 1887
44 × 35
Gift of Mr. Jacques Laroche, subject
to usufruct, 1947 ; admitted in 1963

The remarkable Dr Gachet, who was the author of a thesis on melancholy and a specialist in nervous diseases, was a frequent host to artists at Auvers-sur-Oise. Pissarro, Guillaumin and Cézanne were among his close friends. In June 1890, he took up Van Gogh and cared for him till his suicide in July of the same year. It was while he was with Dr Gachet that the painter created his most expressionist works, such as the poignant *Église d'Auvers*, which is like a cry from the darkness.

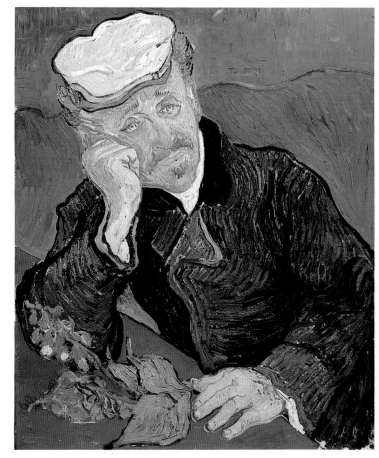

Vincent Van Gogh (1853-1890)
Le Docteur Paul Gachet, 1890
68 × 57
Gift of Paul and Marguerite Gachet
children of the model, 1949

96

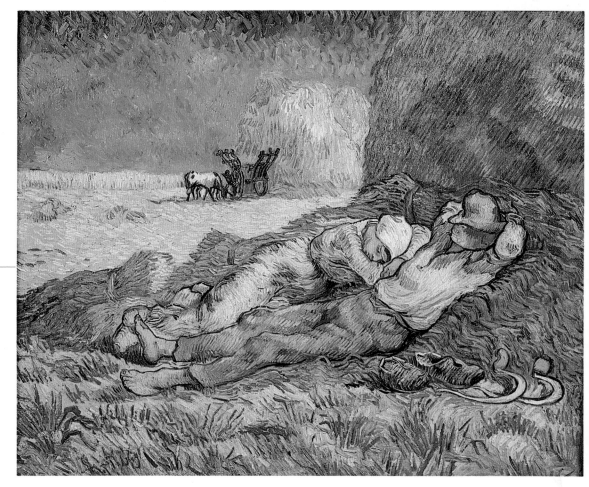

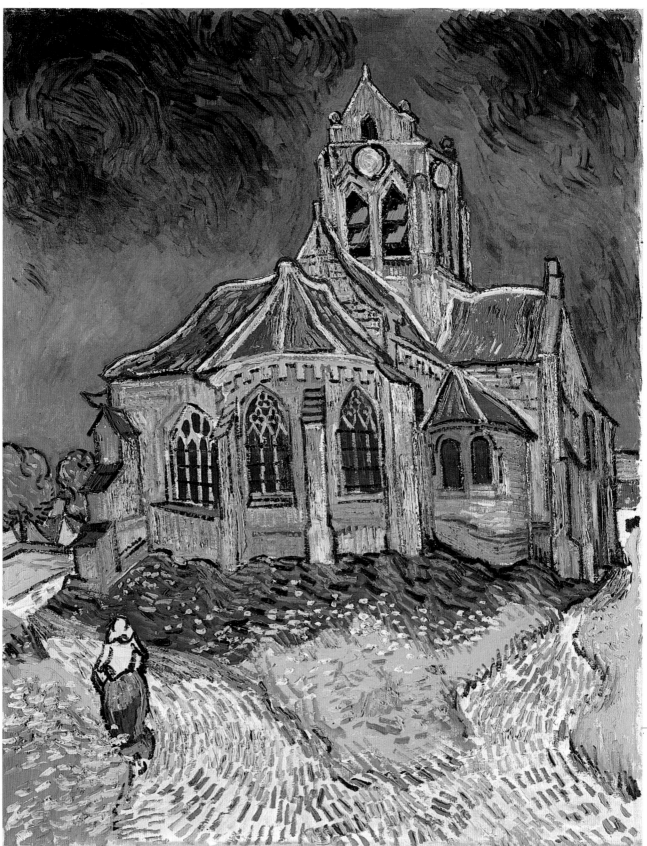

Vincent Van Gogh (1853-1890)
La Méridienne or *La Sieste*, 1889-1890
73 × 91
Painted after a carved scene reproducing a drawing by J.-F. Millet
Gift of Mme Fernand Halphen, subject to usufruct, 1952; admitted in 1963

Vincent Van Gogh (1853-1890)
L'Église d'Auvers-sur-Oise, 1890
94 × 74
Acquired with the cooperation of Paul Gachet and an
anonymous Canadian donation, 1951

These three finished studies for the great painting of *Les Poseuses*, which absorbed the artist's attention from 1886 to 1888, represent the quintessence of Seurat's art. They show a technical virtuosity worthy of a miniaturist, along with implacable scientific rigour; but neither of these qualities excluded the sheer poetry of the figures, with overtones emphasised by Seurat's deeply classical treatment. One may also discern the influence of the scholar Ch. Henry, whose theories on the dynamic of line had a strong effect on the artist in his final years.

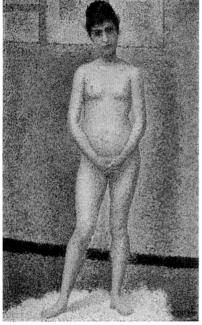

Georges Seurat (1859-1891)
Three studies for *Les Poseuses*, 1886-1887
Wood; size of each panel : 25 × 16
Acquired in 1947

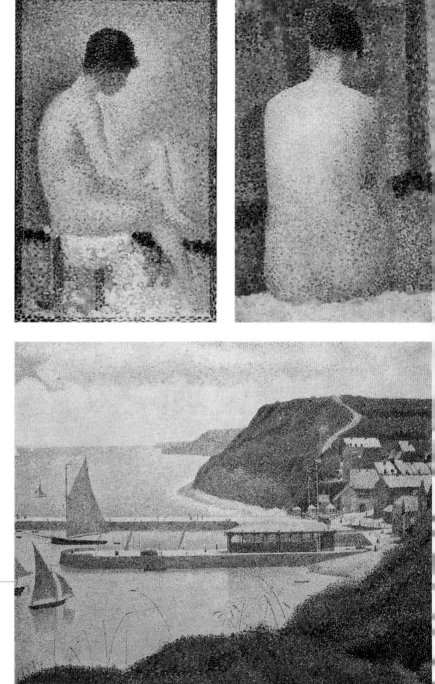

98

Georges Seurat (1859-1891)
Port-en-Bessin, avant-port, marée haute, 1888
67 × 82
Acquired on the arrears of an anonymous
Canadian donation, 1952

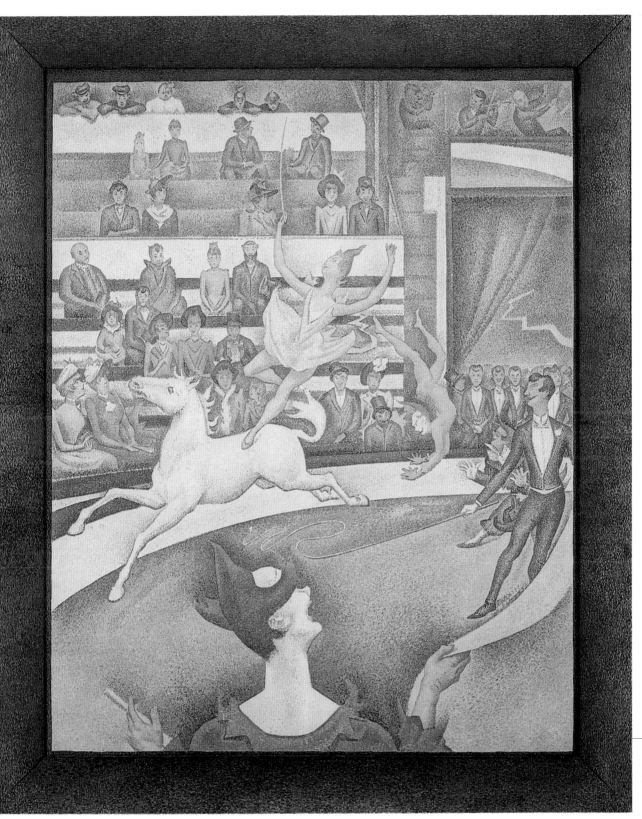

Georges Seurat (1859-1891)
Le Cirque, 1891, unfinished
185 × 152
Salon des Indépendants, 1891
Bequest of John Quinn, 1925

Henri-Edmond Cross (1856-1910)
Les Iles d'or, îles d'Hyères, circa 1891-1892
59 × 54
Acquired in 1947

100

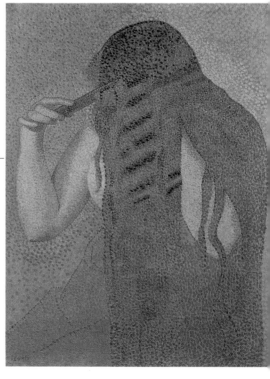

Henri-Edmond Cross (1856-1910)
La Chevelure, circa 1892
61 × 46
Acquired in 1969

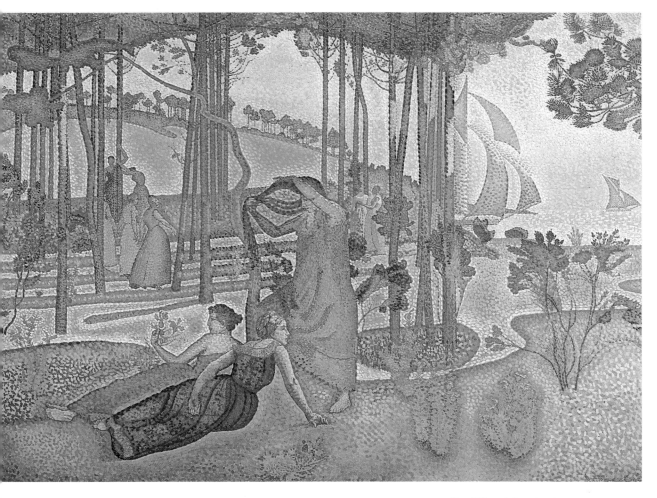

Henri-Edmond Cross (1856-1910)
L'Air du soir, 1893-1894
Salon des Indépendants, 1894
116 × 165
Donation by Ginette Signac
subject to usufruct 1976
usufruct abandoned in 1979

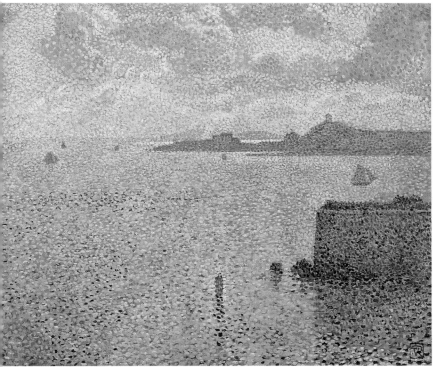

Théo Van Rysselberghe (1862-1926)
Voiliers et estuaire, circa 1892-1893
50 × 61
Acquired in 1982

Having settled in Saint-Tropez in 1892, Signac discovered the South of France where the light transforms shapes and colours. In the *Femmes au puits* he had pushed theoretical research to its extremes, systematically using the laws of simultaneous colour contrasts and optic mix in a way which prefigured Seurat. Signac found a new spontaneity in the progressive enlargement of his touch, of which *La Bouée rouge* is a striking example.

Luce's fan is of a more decorative character, painted in a fine pointillist technique. It shows one of the views of Paris of which he was so fond, sparkling in the night.

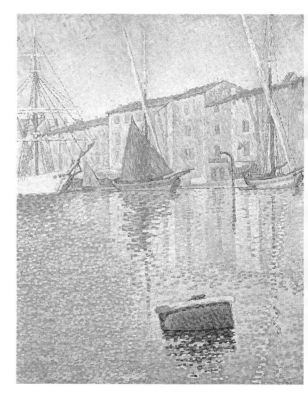

Paul Signac (1863-1935)
La Bouée rouge, 1895
81 × 65
Gift of Dr Pierre Hébert, subject to usufruct, 1957
admitted in 1973

102

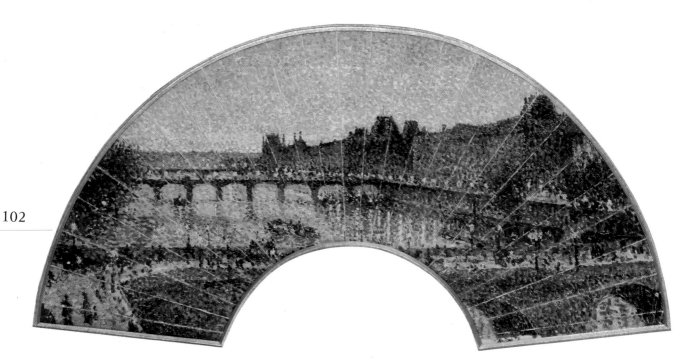

Maximilien Luce (1858-1941)
The Louvre and The Pont-neuf at night,
c. 1890-1892
18,5 × 56,5
Gift from Madame Ginette Signac,
subject to usufruct, in 1976.

Paul Signac (1863-1935)
Jeunes Provençales au puits, 1892
Salon des Indépendants, 1893
(decoration for a panel)
195 × 131
Acquired in 1979

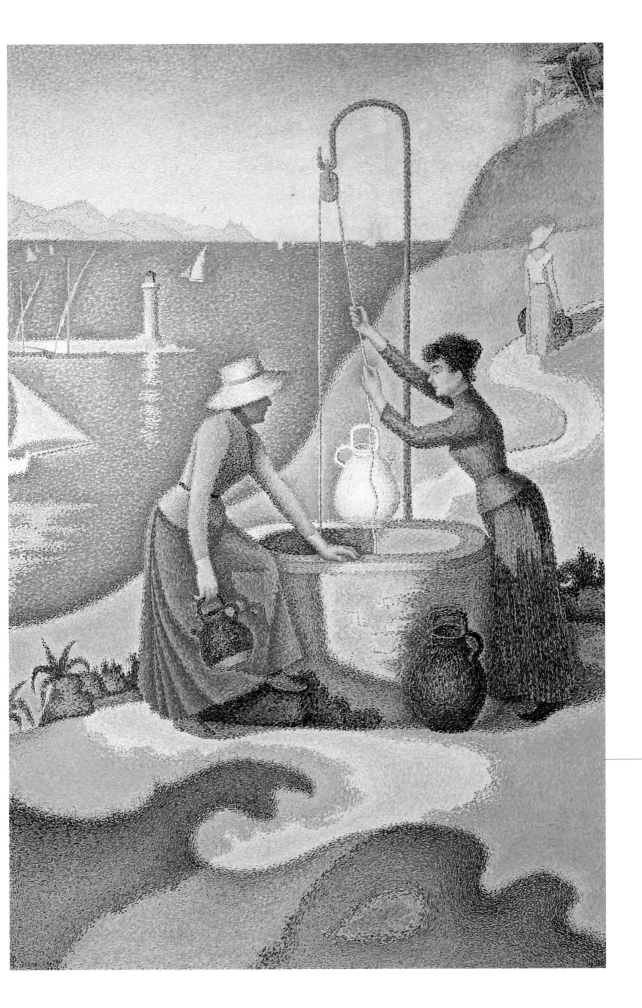

103

104

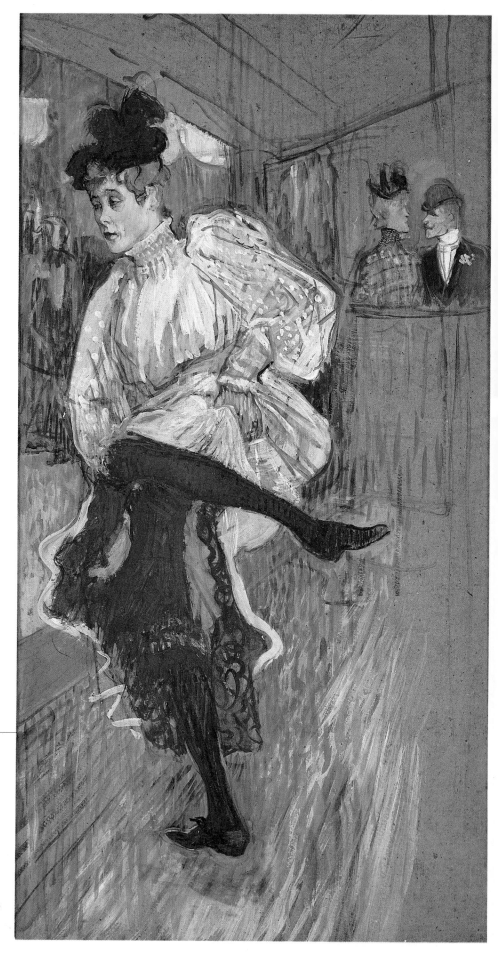

Henri de Toulouse-Lautrec (1864-1901)
Jane Avril dansant, circa 1892
Hardboard, 85 × 45
Bequest of Antonin Personnaz, 1937

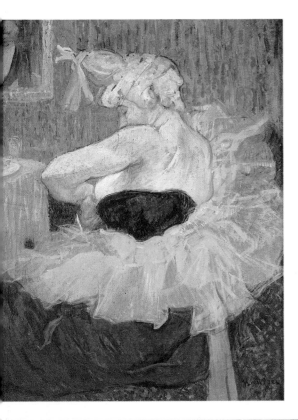

Henri de Toulouse-Lautrec (1864-1901)
La Clownesse Cha-u-Kao, 1895
Hardboard, 64 × 49
Bequest of Isaac de Camondo, 1911

iving chronicle of Paris with its brothels and cabarets, the work of Toulouse-Lautrec brings to life the stars of the stage and quadrille. *Jane Avril* is here sketched from life at the Moulin Rouge, while the *Clownesse Cha-u-Kao* straightens her costume in her dressing room : both are rendered with stunning virtuosity. When la Goulue left for the Foire du trône at Neuilly, she asked her friend to decorate the booth in which she was to do her new act. This he did, with two large canvases, one of la Goulue as a dancing girl, the other in company with her famous partner Valentin le Désossé.

Henri de Toulouse-Lautrec (1864-1901)
La Danse mauresque or *Les Almées*
Panel for la Goulue's booth, 1895
285 × 307
Acquired in fragments in 1929, later restored

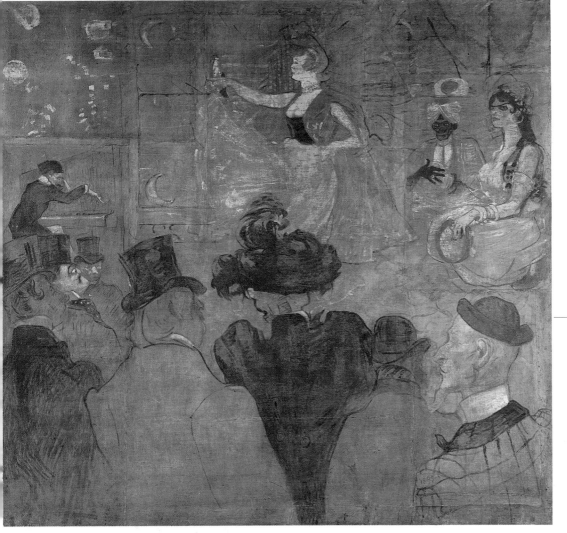

105

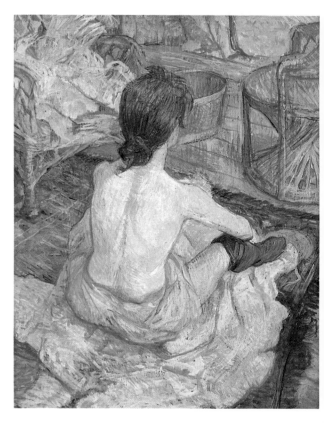

Henri de Toulouse-Lautrec (1864-1901)
La Toilette, 1896
Hardboard, 67 × 54
Bequest of Pierre Goujon, 1914

Henri de Toulouse-Lautrec (1864-1901)
Le Lit, circa 1892
Hardboard on parqueted panel, 54 × 70
Bequest of Antonin Personnaz, 1937

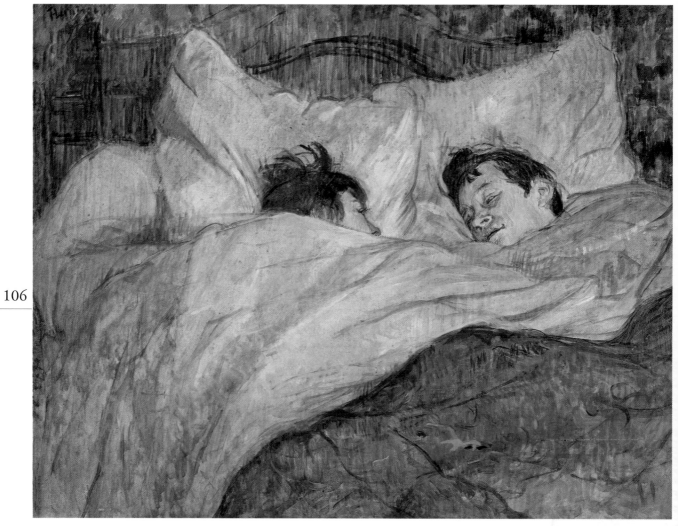

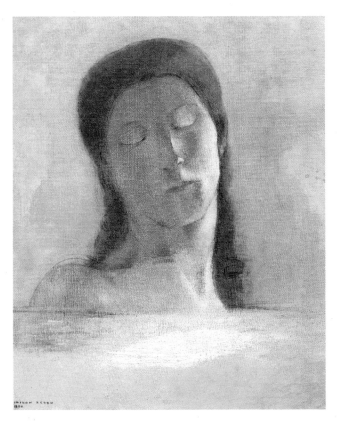

Odilon Redon (1840-1916)
Les Yeux clos, 1890
44 × 36
Acquired in 1904

Odilon Redon (1840-1916)
La Coquille, 1912
Pastel, 52 × 57
Bequest of Mme Ari Redon, 1984

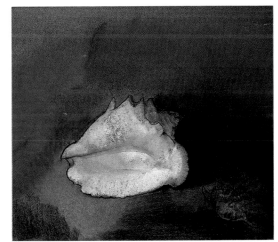

107

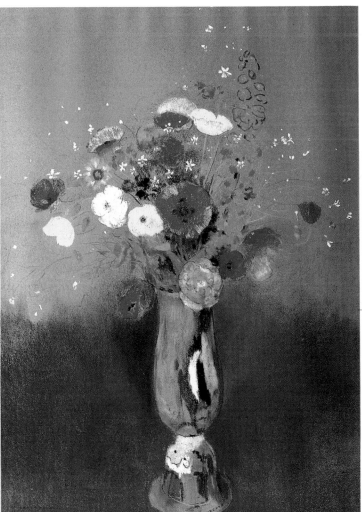

Odilon Redon (1840-1916)
Bouquet de fleurs des champs, circa 1912
Pastel, 57 × 35
Gift of the Société des Amis du Louvre, 1954

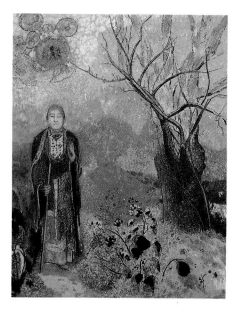

Odilon Redon (1840-1916)
Le Bouddha, circa 1905
Pastel, 90 × 73
Acquired in 1971

Seduced by the new ideas (modelled on the Nabi painters) for the revitalization of interior design, in 1899 Redon threw himself into a vast series of paintings intended for the dining room of the château de Domecy, in the Yonne.

Arbres sur fond jaune is one of seven large panels, complementing eight smaller ones, which formed this series, completed in October 1901. Here Redon uses, in an entirely personal way, his research into chromatic harmony, blending flora and fauna, both real and imaginary.

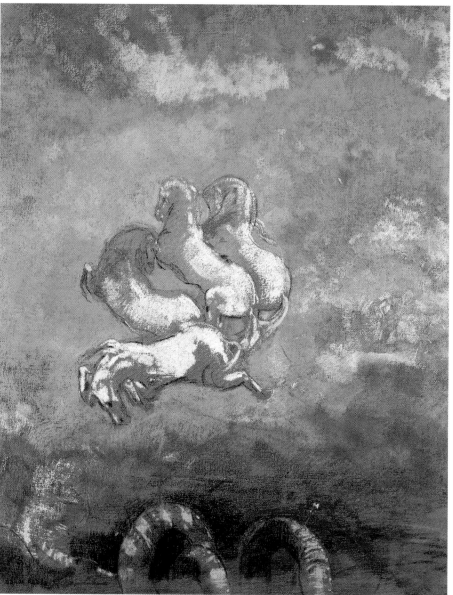

Odilon Redon (1840-1916)
Le Char d'Apollon, 1905-1914
Pastel, 91 × 77
Acquired by dation in 1978

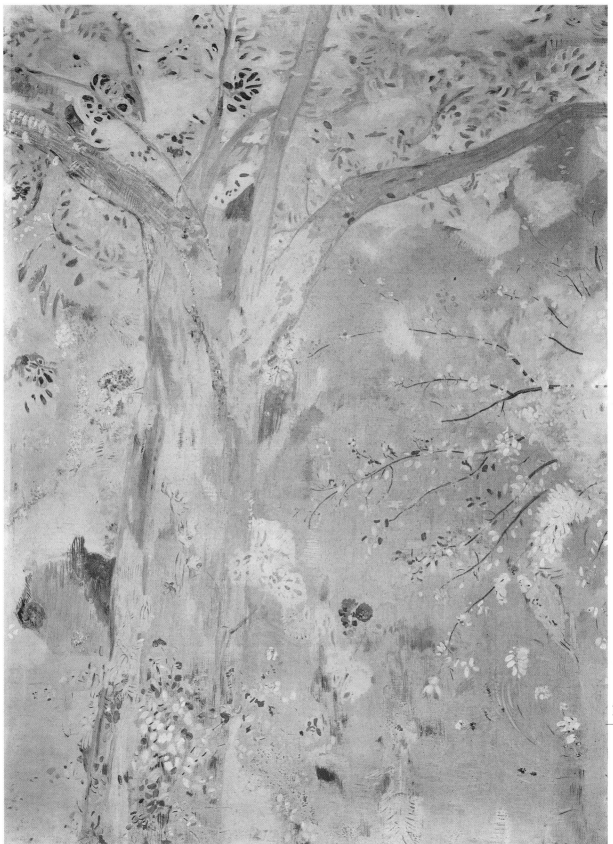

Odilon Redon
Arbre sur fond jaune, 1901
249 × 185
Acquired by dation in 1988

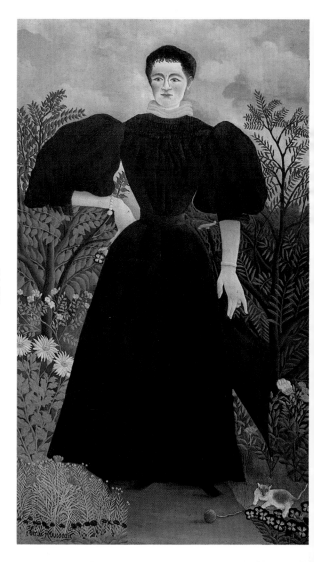

Henri Rousseau, known as le Douanier (1844-1910)
Portrait de femme, circa 1897
198 × 114
Donation of Baroness Eva Gebhard-Gourgaud, 1965

Henri Rousseau, known as le Douanier (1844-1910)
La Guerre or *La Chevauchée de la Discorde*
Salon des Indépendants, 1894
114 × 195
Acquired in 1946

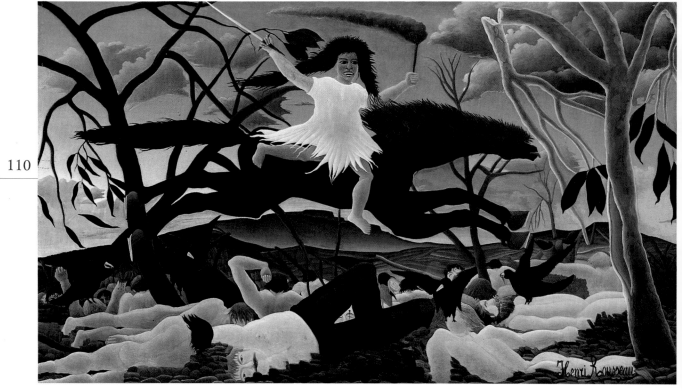

D ouanier Rousseau is a figure who is hard to classify. He was a self-taught painter, who for years remained an amateur, and he liked to claim artistic kinship with the conventional Gérôme. Nonetheless, he had a strong taste for paradox, and probably the only label which can be ascribed to him is that of independant. Rousseau drew his inspiration from the images of Epinal, old photographs and visits to the jardin des Plantes in Paris; he would then apply his imagination to what he had seen, creating a bizarre, symbolic world that was all his own. Rousseau's mystery is clothed in the false ingenuousness of the naive and framed by lush decoration.

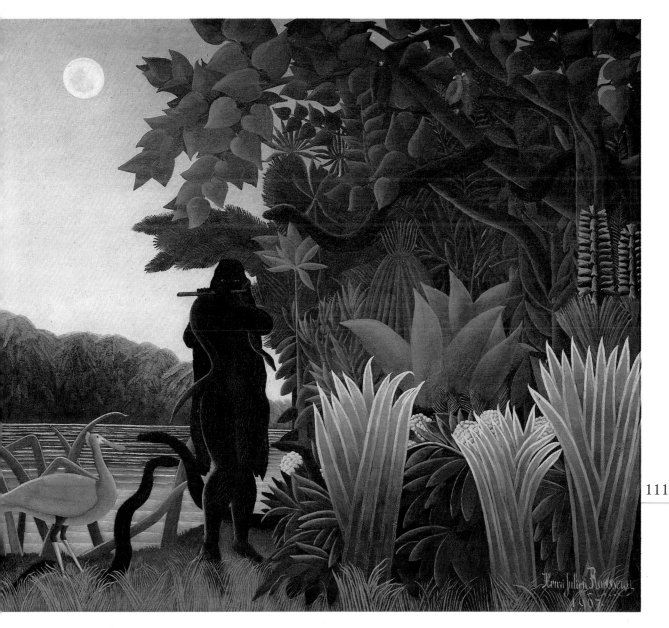

Henri Rousseau, known as le Douanier (1844-1910)
La Charmeuse de serpents
Salon d'automne, 1907
169 × 189
Bequest of Jacques Doucet, 1936

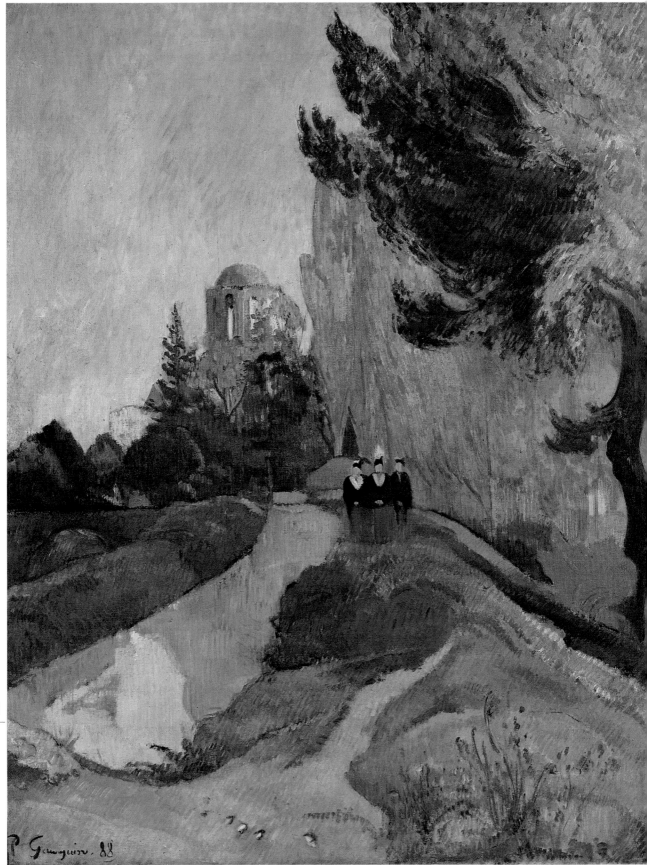

112

Paul Gauguin (1848-1903)
Les Alyscamps, Arles, 1888
91 × 72
Gift of countess Vitali in memory of her father
viscount Guy du Cholet, 1923 ; admitted in 1938

Vincent Van Gogh (1853-1890)
L'Arlésienne, Mme Ginoux, 1888
92 × 73
Gift of Mme de Goldschmidt-Rothschild, August 1944
subject to usufruct ; admitted in 1974

At the request of Van Gogh, who dreamed of founding an "atelier du Midi", Gauguin stayed with him at Arles at the end of 1888. This stay produced a number of fruitful exchanges between the two artists, who influenced each other strongly and deliberately painted the same subjects for comparison. Thus on several occasions Van Gogh painted the alley to the Arles cemetery of Les Alyscamps and Mme Ginoux, the *Arlésienne* of whom Van Gogh did two different versions, appears in a Gauguin canvas entitled *Au café*. The dramatic episode of the cutting-off of Van Gogh's ear brought this experiment to an end.

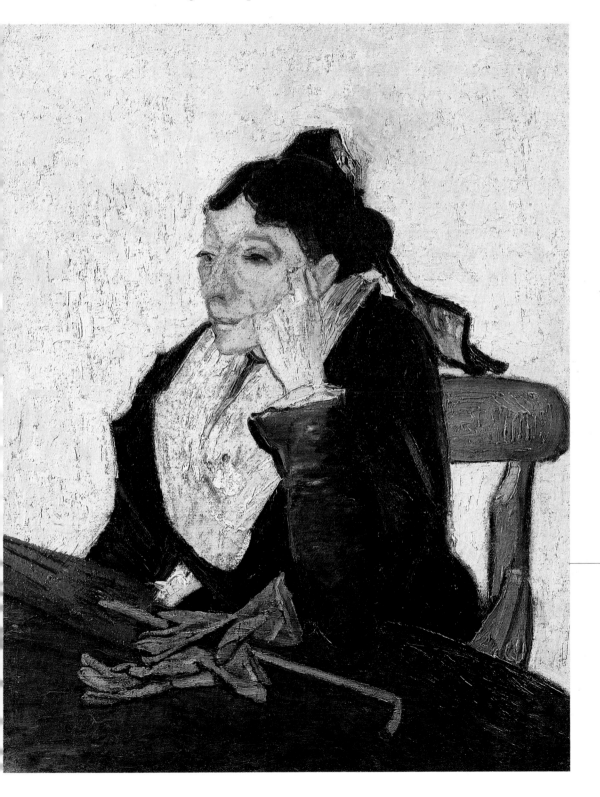

113

Paul Sérusier (1864-1927)
Le Talisman, 1888
Wood, 27 x 21
Acquired with the participation of
Philippe Meyer through the Lutèce Foundation, 1985

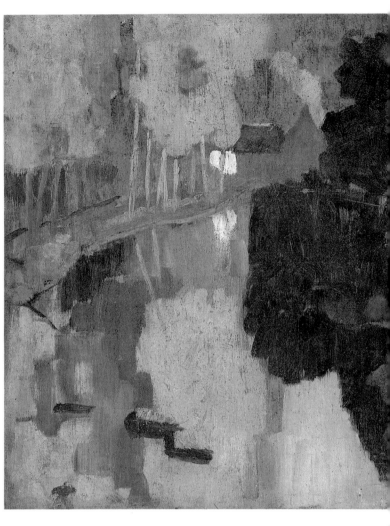

Émile Bernard (1868-1941)
Madeleine au bois d'Amour, Madeleine Bernard
the artist's sister, 1888
138 × 163
Acquired in 1977

114

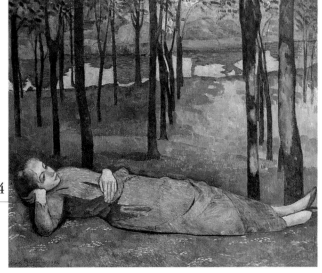

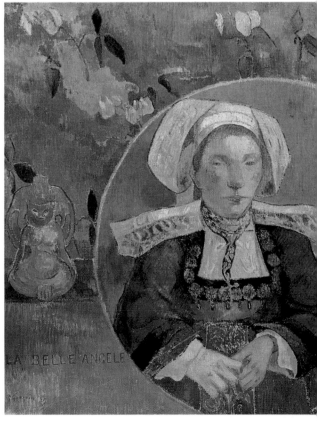

Paul Gauguin (1848-1903)
La Belle Angèle, Mme Satre, hotelkeeper at Pont-Aven, 1889
92 × 73
Gift of Ambroise Vollard, 1927

How do you see that tree?, Gauguin is reported to have said at the corner of the bois d'Amour. Is it green? Well, use green, the most beautiful green on your palette; and that shadow, it's more blue than anything else. So paint it as blue as you possibly can." Serusier's *Talisman* epitomises Gauguin's lesson, but it is first and foremost a declaration of the liberty to dare anything, a liberty which demolished all the old constraints of realism and proclaims the autonomy of the thing painted.

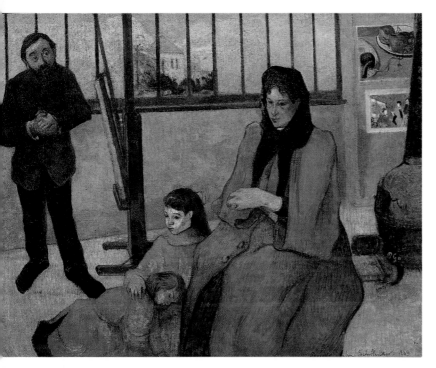

Paul Gauguin (1848-1903)
La Famille Schuffenecker, 1889
73 × 92
Former Matsukata collection; admitted in 1959
in accordance with the peace treaty with Japan

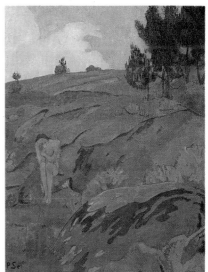

Paul Sérusier (1864-1927)
Ève bretonne or *Mélancolie*, circa 1890
72 × 58
Donation of Henriette Boutaric, subject to usufruct, 1980
admitted in 1983

115

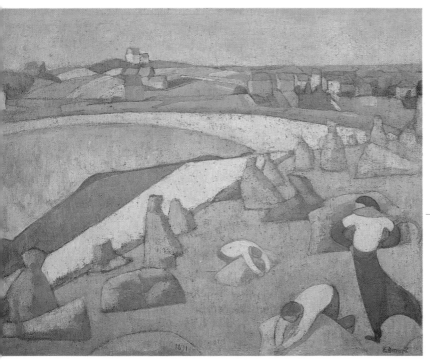

Émile Bernard (1868-1941)
La Moisson au bord de la mer, 1892
70 × 92
Acquired in 1982

Paul Gauguin (1848-1903)
Femmes de Tahiti or *Sur la plage*, 1891
69 × 91
Bequest of viscount Guy du Cholet, 1923

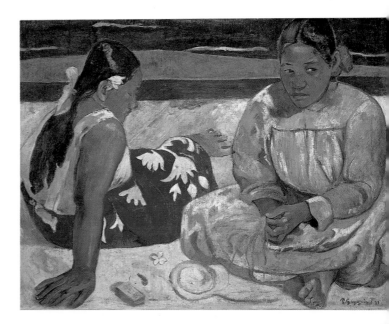

Paul Gauguin (1848-1903)
Le Repas, 1891
73 × 92
Donation of M. and Mme André Meyer
subject to usufruct, 1954
usufruct abandoned in 1975

116

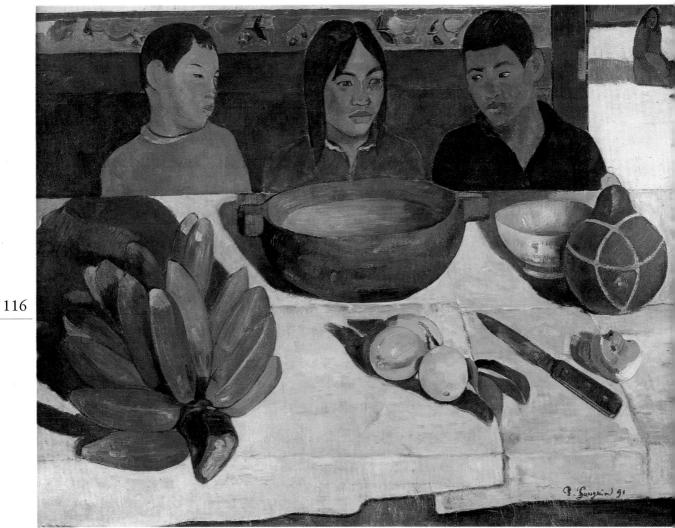

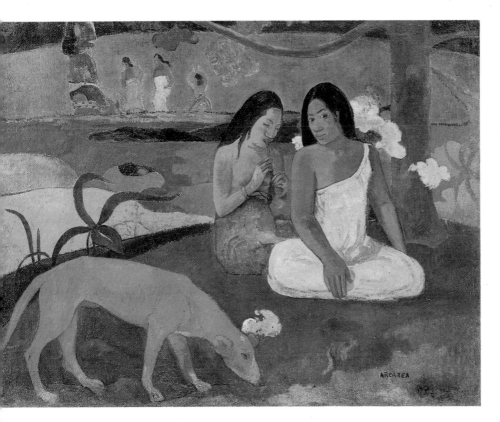

Paul Gauguin (1848-1903)
Arearea (Joyeusetés), 1892
75 × 94
Bequest of M. and Mme Lung, 1961

Paul Gauguin (1848-1903)
Portrait de l'artiste, 1896
40 × 32
Dedicated to his *friend Daniel*
Gift of Mme Huc de Monfreid, 1951
admitted in 1968

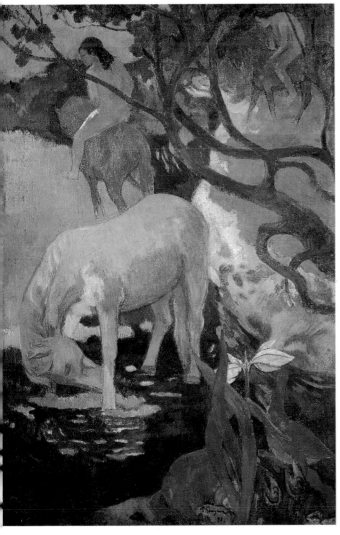

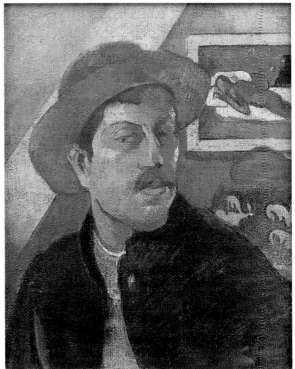

Paul Gauguin (1848-1903)
Le Cheval blanc, 1898
140 × 91
Acquired in 1927

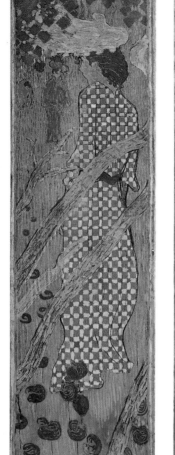
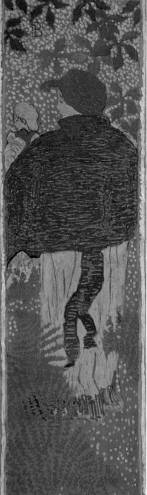
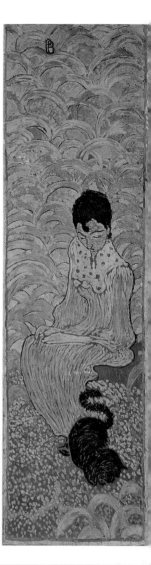

Pierre Bonnard (1867-1947)
Femmes au jardin, 1891
Salon des Indépendants, 1891
Size of each panel : 160 × 48
Acquired by dation in 1984

118

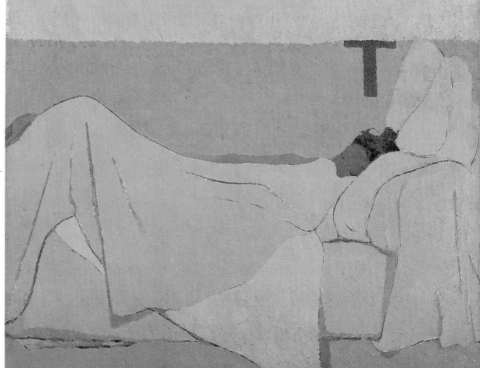

Édouard Vuillard (1868-1940)
Au lit, 1891
73 × 92
Verbal bequest of the artist executed by
M. and Mme Ker-Xavier Roussel, 1941

Bonnard's *Femmes au jardin* was first intended as a screen, but the four panels were separated by Bonnard himself when he exhibited them at the 1891 Salon des Indépendants. The following year, he presented *Crépuscule* (or *La Partie de croquet*) at this same Salon, a painting which perfectly summarises his Nabi experiments : the renunciation of traditional notions of space under the joint influence of Japanese art, Gauguin and the practice of theatre décors ; flat, sinuous figures without relief, decorative exuberance and compositions based on contrasting values. At the same time, Vuillard's *Au lit* offered a more ascetic version of the nabi principles, in a monochromatic painting of flat tints based on a subtly simplified geometrical structure.

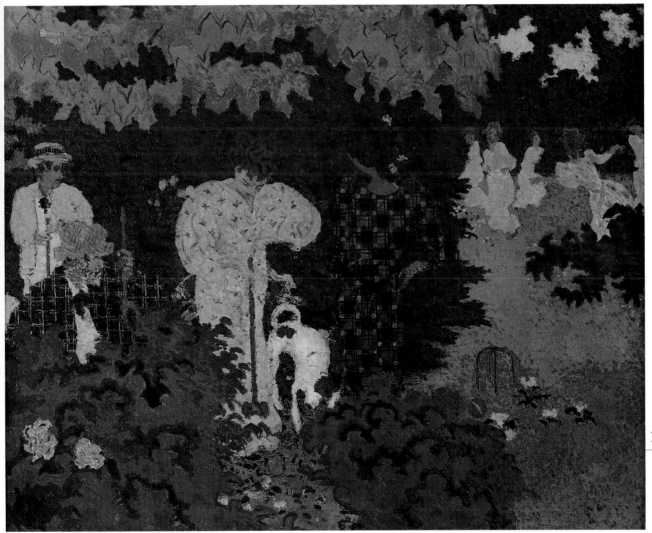

119

Pierre Bonnard (1867-1947)
Crépuscule or *La Partie de croquet*
Salon des Indépendants, 1892
130 × 162
Gift of M. de Wildenstein through the Société
des Amis du musée d'Orsay, 1985

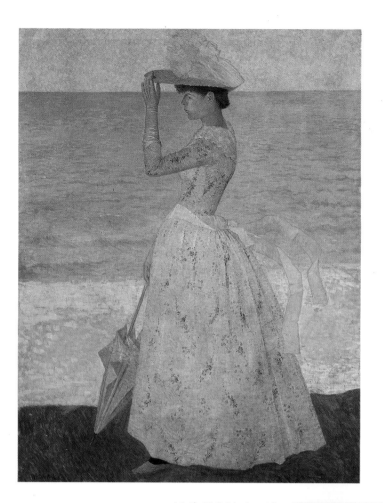

Aristide Maillol (1861-1944)
La Femme à l'ombrelle
190 × 149
Acquired in 1955

In 1894, Vuillard painted one of his first decorative ensembles for the private townhouse of Alexandre Natanson. Out of the nine original panels, the Musée d'Orsay now possesses five, all executed in glue-based paint whose mattness has fortunately been preserved. The composition is based on the alternation of dark and clear masses and a rhythmic train of images emphasised by the continuity of sinuous lines. The influence of Puvis de Chavannes is very strong here, as in *Les Muses* and *La Femme à l'ombrelle*, in which the decorative aspect controls the internal economy of the canvas.

120

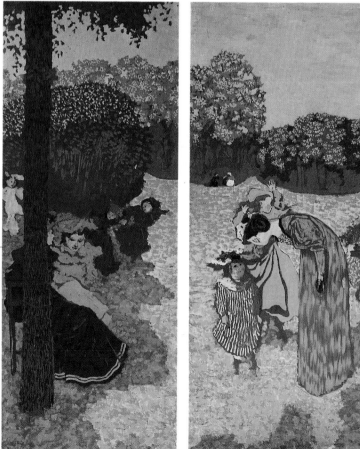

Édouard Vuillard (1868-1940)
Jardins publics, decoration for Alexandre Natanson, 1894
Fillettes jouant, 214 × 88
L'Interrogatoire, 214 × 92
Bequest of Mme Alexandre Radot, 1978

Les Nourrices, 213 × 73
La Conversation, 213 × 154
L'Ombrelle rouge, 213 × 81
Acquired for the Musée du Luxembourg, 1929

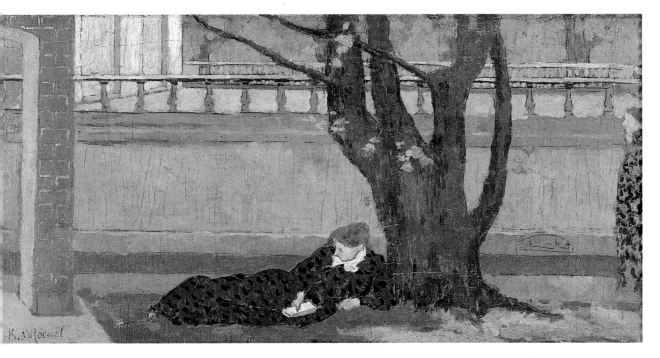

Ker-Xavier Roussel (1867-1944)
La Terrasse, c. 1892
36 × 75
Acquired in 1992

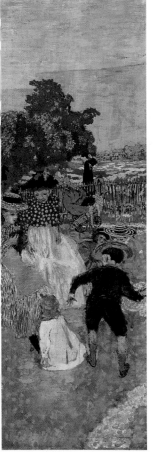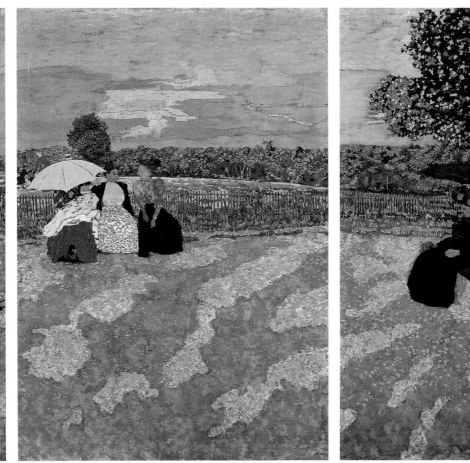

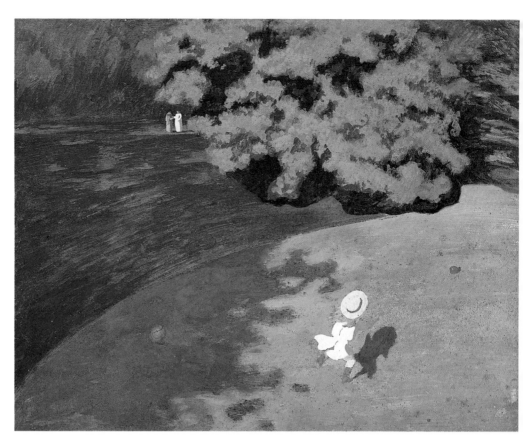

Félix Valloton (1865-1925)
Le Ballon, 1899
Hardboard, 48 × 61
Bequest of Carle Dreyfus, 1953

122

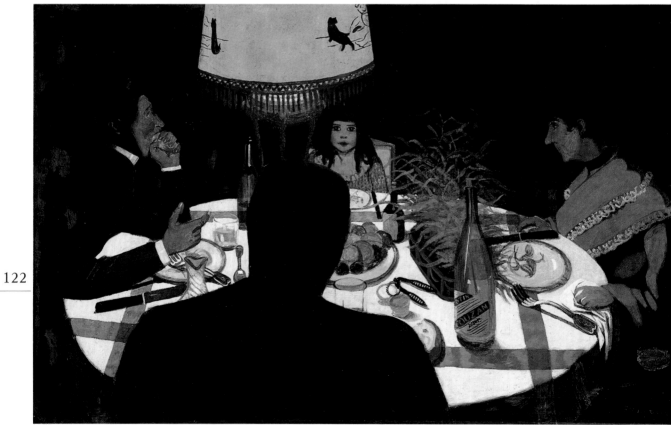

Félix Vallotton (1865-1925)
Le Dîner, effet de lampe, 1899
Wood, 57 × 89
Acquired in 1947

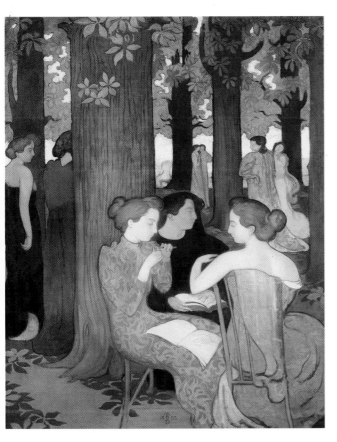

Maurice Denis (1870-1943)
Les Muses, 1893
171 × 137
Salon des Indépendants, 1893
Acquired in 1932

A group portrait like those of Fantin-Latour, *L'Hommage à Cézanne* shows (from left to right) : Odilon Redon, Vuillard, the critic André Mellerio, Ambroise Vollard, Maurice Denis, Sérusier, Ranson, Roussel, Bonnard and Marthe Denis, the artist's wife. The group surrounds a still life by Cézanne which once belonged to Gauguin, in Ambroise Vollard's shop in the rue Laffitte.

Maurice Denis (1870-1943)
Hommage à Cézanne, 1900
Salon of Société nationale des Beaux-Arts, 1901
180 × 240
Gift of André Gide, 1928

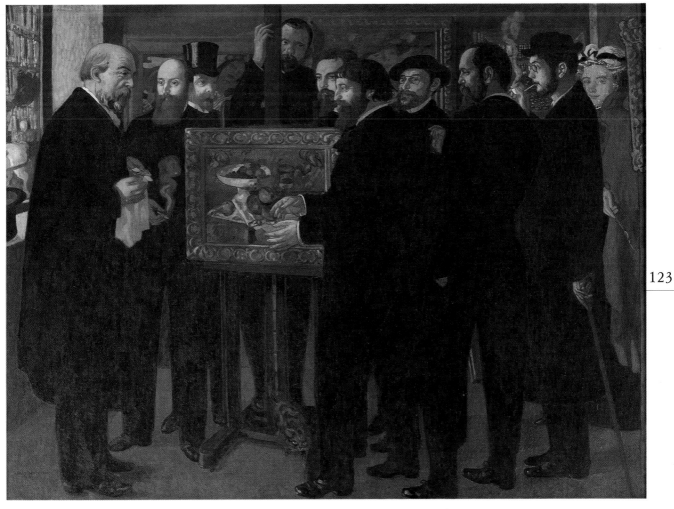

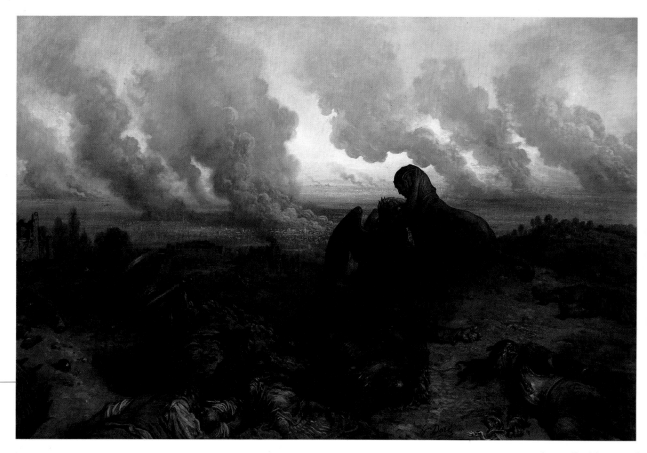

Gustave Doré (1832-1883)
L'Énigme, 1871
130 × 195,5
Acquired in 1982

Naturalism and symbolism

The events that marked the fall of the Second Empire, the war of 1870, the siege of Paris and the Commune, were in no wise reflected in the collections of the Musée du Luxembourg. Indeed, everything happened so suddenly that few artists had time to be greatly inspired. Nonetheless, Gustave Doré, who remained in Paris, witnessed scenes which prompted some extraordinary drawings from life, along with several allegorical paintings; these included *L'Enigme*, acquired recently by the Musée d'Orsay. At the posthumous sale of Doré's work in 1885, this painting was grouped with *L'Aigle noir de Prusse* and *La Défense de Paris* in a sequence entitled *Souvenir de 1870*. Two lines written by Victor Hugo in 1837 were associated with L'Énigme :
"O spectacle, ainsi meurt ce que les peuples font!
Qu'un tel passé pour l'âme est un gouffre profond."
Backed by a blazing city—Paris, without a doubt—the civilian and military victims of the conflict surround the weeping image of France, personified by a winged woman who interrogates a sphinx as to the reasons for the disaster.

A large number of Meissonier sketches came to the Musée du Luxembourg from an 1898 bequest by the artist's widow and an earlier gift from his son Charles; among them was an impressive study for *Le Siège de Paris*. This painting was feverishly executed in Meissonier's Poissy studio, in the heat of his rage at France's defeat; his Paris house had been requisitioned by the enemy. "That was my vengeance", Meissonier wrote later in his *Entretiens*. One of the identifiable figures in the picture is the painter Regnault, who is seen collapsing beside a monumental image representing the city of Paris, which stands before the national flag draped in a lionskin. This giantess makes the whole painting into an allegory : without her, it would consist of nothing other than war images such as were produced in vast numbers after 1880 by chroniclers of military life like Edward Detaille.

Meissonier, who was basically a specialist in smaller formats, dreamed of developing this sketch into a full-blown painting, but never did so; likewise, he died before completing the State commission for the Panthéon engineered on his behalf by Philippe de Chennevières. The plan for the Panthéon was conceived in 1874 and drawn up in 1875; in it, Meissonier was given the task of painting another siege of Paris, that of the Franks, which resulted in the famine of St. Geneviève's time.

Puvis de Chavannes, who between 1875 and 1878 had successfully completed his Panthéon sequence depicting the childhood of St. Geneviève, was appointed to succeed Meissonier, in preference to Detaille. The work was done between 1893 and 1898, the year of Puvis' death. By that time the rules of the Musée du Luxembourg had been relaxed, and some sketches by Puvis were acquired, including *Sainte Geneviève ravitaillant Paris*. Here Puvis avoided scenes of the famine, preferring to show the patron saint of Paris in the process of relieving the citizens' hunger.

Many of the great Second Empire décors vanished in the fires of the Commune. Under the Third Republic, private commissions proliferated, but

125

few have survived; the recent salvage of Luc-Olivier Merson's work for the hôtel Watel-Delaynin is an exception. Public commissions, too, were frequent for the decoration of buildings of every sort, particularly town halls and theatres. The plaster maquette for the ceiling of the Comédie-Française by Albert Besnard has survived intact, but it was only by a lucky recent purchase that the Museum was able to acquire Benjamin Constant's first sketch for the ceiling of the Opéra-Comique. There was even a plan to decorate the railway stations; it was an old unrealised dream of Courbet's to contribute to such a project. In 1900, the more academic artists (Gabriel Ferrier, Benjamin Constant and Pierre Fritel) took part in the decoration of the hôtel Terminus beside the Gare d'Orsay, while Fernand Cormon painted landscapes for the main hall of the station. One of these may still be seen behind another of Cormon's compositions, one of the glories of the last official Salon in 1880 which at the time was immediately acquired for the Musée du Luxembourg : *Caïn*, the first "prehistoric" subject ever tackled by the artist. In fact, this monumental work refers to some verses of "La conscience", from *La Légende des siècles* by Victor Hugo, who had been proscribed by the man he had christened "Napoléon le Petit" but had now returned in triumph to republican France. Cormon has used the traditional procedures of academic art in *Caïn*; indeed, his contemporaries took a delight in identifying certain professional models in the painting's hairy fugitives. Nonetheless, it is clear that he has already assimilated certain characteristics of naturalist painting, which at that time were dominant, along with every possible variation of official art at the commencement in 1880 of the Third Republic. Those who had been ill-treated under the Second Empire were now much glorified (though some, of course, were dead). The prices of Millet's paintings rose sharply; the École des Beaux-Arts organised a Courbet exhibition in 1882 and a Manet exhibition in 1883; Jules Bastien-Lepage, who died aged 36 in 1884, was given a retrospective of his work a few months after his death at the Hôtel de Chimay, at which the administration chose to acquire a large painting entitled *Les Foins* for the Musée du Luxembourg. This purchase effectively added a naturalist work with life-size figures to the collection, which provided a link both in scale and subject matter with the proclamation paintings of 1849-1850 while also containing overtones of impressionist techniques.

Naturalist painting as a genre was especially attached to rustic themes (another famous example is Léon Lhermitte's *La Paye des moissonneurs*) and the world of modern industry (as in Cormon's *La Forge*, and *Au pays noir* by the Belgian painter Constantin Meunier, both produced at the turn of the century). Yet no sooner was naturalism established in the full glare of official approval, than it began to be questioned by those who, like Joséphin Péladan, the future manager of the Rose-Croix Salons, saw it as a symbol of decadence in art caused by a lack of idealism and spirituality. Vulgarised naturalism, with its quickly-applied colours, began to be perceived as an easy way of painting. It was used for every theme, including those of religion and symbolism, and it invaded every country in Europe, most of which had less suffocating academic structures than did France. The stronger artistic personalities adopted a fine and vigorous brand of naturalism, like the Dutch painter Breitner (represented at the Musée d'Orsay by a recent purchase), or the German, Liebermann. Between 1870 and 1880 the latter artist painted a large number of subjects drawn from the working world, probably even more than his French counterparts; and there is little doubt that he visited

Paris and perhaps Barbizon during this period. Liebermann also had the remarkable example of painters such as Menzel, who unfortunately for us belonged to a generation too old to have been represented in the Luxembourg, despite the presence of his striking *Rolling Mill* at the 1878 Universal Exhibition. Later, in 1895, when the Musée du Luxembourg was finally taking an interest in foreign artists, Liebermann's *Biergasten at Brannenburg* (1893) was acquired. Here, the theme is somewhat more pleasant. The canvas is bright and clear, with special attention given to atmospheric and light effects; hence the work seems more post-impressionist than naturalist, since naturalist paintings often tend to be swamped in an unvarying, leaden light.

The sphere of portraiture shows clearly how techniques evolved from Bonnat or Delaunay's sombre, serious effigies to the brilliant work of Sargent. For instance, the picture of *Édouard Pailleron* (1879) by Sargent is executed with daring freedom, while Albert Besnard's *Portrait de Madame Roger Jourdain* makes full and fresh use of an artificial yellow light. Other pioneers included Jacques-Emile Blanche, and Boldini, a virtuoso at rapid brushwork.

As always, most portraits tended to remain in the family of the person who commissioned them, only reaching museums many years later, usually in the form of a donation. This was the case of a portrait by the Russian painter Sérov, *Madame Lwoff*, most delicately executed in nabi tones.

As a reaction to naturalism, symbolist tendencies began to appear in the ranks of both the post-impressionists and among non avant-garde painters, the symbolist manifesto being published in 1886. The younger generation now looked to some of their elders, and found that while Moreau and Puvis de Chavannes each had a remarkable work in the Musée du Luxembourg, Burne-Jones was absent (apart from some drawings given by the artist himself), and Böcklin had been totally ignored. At that time, the museum was no longer playing its allotted rôle of displaying model works for contemporary artists. On the contrary, those models now had to be searched for in the exhibitions that proliferated outside the museum, as well as in illustrated books and periodicals.

Thus the Musée d'Orsay's collection of important works by the above artists are of recent acquisition. In the case of Burne-Jones, the opportunity missed at the close of the 19th century has been made good by the purchase of a major work admired by Puvis de Chavannes, part of a French private collection for the last fifty years. As to Böcklin, one of his classical compositions has lately been recovered, a work not unrelated to Paul Huet's *Le Gouffre*, which also is a recent acquisition.

Among the first discreetly symbolist works to enter the Luxembourg was a delicate portrait of *Thadée Jacquet* by Aman-Jean, one of a group devoted to the Salon de la Rose Croix and to the new Société nationale des Beaux-Arts. Also admitted were works by Carrière, whose immense *Famille du peintre* was brought in 1897. More to the modern taste, perhaps, are his attractive *L'Enfant au verre*, or his portraits of writers, especially the famous rendering of the poet Paul Verlaine, acquired in 1910 with the help of the Société des Amis du Luxembourg. It is essentially thanks to various donations (of which the most abundant were those of Carrière's friend, the sculptor Devillez, in 1930, and the recent bequest of his son-in-law, Ivan Loiseau), that this artist is so well represented in the Musée d'Orsay. Nevertheless, Carrière remains a little-known figure in fin-de-siècle symbolism. In confining himself more and more strictly to a range of browns, he drew away from Ribot's brand of realism in the 1880s to arrive at a simple play of curves controlling a few light-filled zones. This had the effect of producing a kind of dreamy magic, both in the intimist scenes where the artist relates, without anecdote, certain essential aspects of life, and in his sinuous, almost Art Nouveau landscapes.

Most of the symbolists of the 1890 vintage gradually moved away from their early naturalism; this shift was especially notable in the case of Léon Frédéric, one of the few foreigners of that generation to be represented at the Musée du Luxembourg by several works, among them two important symbolist triptychs (one purchased, the other donated). Frédéric had the sympathy of Léonce Bénédite, whose taste around 1900 can be deduced from the fact that he was a fervent supporter of Charles Cottet, the austere, powerful painter of the "Bande noire". Cottet had exhibited work at Le Barc de Boutteville gallery, along with the nabis before they began to attract attention. Seurat remained conspicuously absent for a long time to come; by contrast, his imitators of the Italian divisionist school were well-represented after 1910 thanks to a series of fruitful contacts with the organisers of the Venice Biennale. But 1910 was too late for Segantini, who died on the eve of the 1900 Universal Exhibition, in which many of his works were prominently featured.

Neither the members of the groupe des XX, which had welcomed Seurat and Gauguin to Brussels, nor the artists of the Free Aesthetic, who were probably thought too violent, had any such good fortune. Hence it is only because of recent purchases that the Belgian Khnopff and the Dutchman Toorop, are finally represented at Orsay: the latter, by a painting originally exchanged with Maurice Denis.

In the eruption of artistic changes that marked the close of the century, however wide the Luxembourg opened its doors it could never be more than the privileged instrument of official art. We learn much from its choices about the relationship between art and the administration around 1900. It has been the rôle of more recent acquisitions and donations (enabling the Musée d'Orsay to offer a brilliant selection of works by artists such as Lévy-Dhurmer of Mucha, who were not unsuccessful at the time) to complete and vary the Luxembourg's narrower representation.

Alphonse de Neuville (1835-1885)
Le Cimetière de Saint-Privat, 18 août 1871
Salon des Artistes français, 1881
235,5 × 341
Gift of Roland Knoedler, 1904

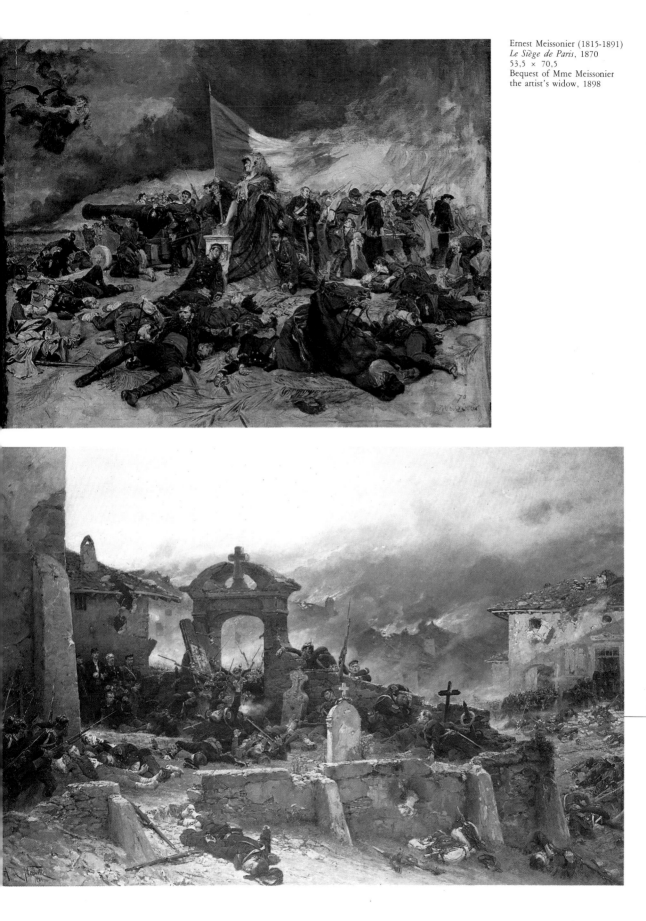

Ernest Meissonier (1815-1891)
Le Siège de Paris, 1870
53,5 × 70,5
Bequest of Mme Meissonier
the artist's widow, 1898

129

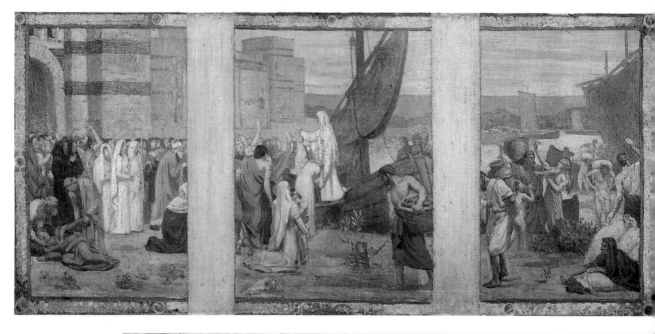

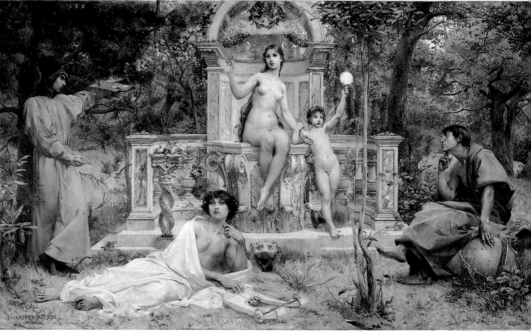

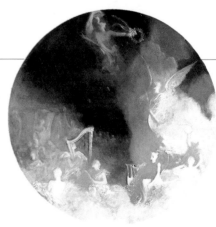

130

Pierre Puvis de Chavannes (1824-1898)
Sainte Geneviève ravitaillant Paris
Sketch for the decoration of the Panthéon
Commissioned in 1896, completed in 1898
64 × 140
Admitted to the Musée du Luxembourg in 1898

Luc-Olivier Merson (1846-1920)
La Vérité
Decoration of stairs of hôtel Watel-Déhaynin, 1901
221 × 372
Acquired when the building was demolished in 1974

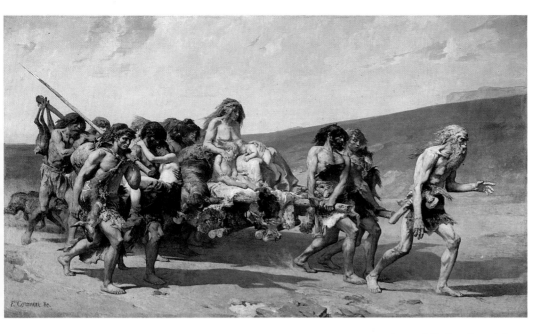

Fernand Cormon (1845-1924)
Caïn, 1880 Salon
384 × 700
Acquired in 1880

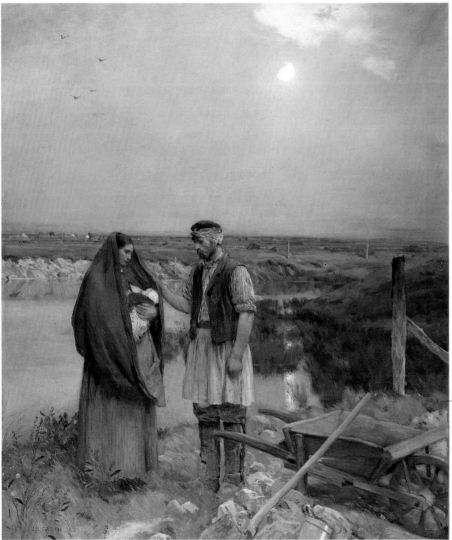

131

Jean-Charles Cazin (1841-1901)
La Journée faite
Salon des Artistes français, 1888
199 × 166
Acquired in 1888

Benjamin Constant (1845-1902)
Glorification de la musique
First sketch for the ceiling of the Opéra-Comique, Paris, painted in 1898
Diameter: 56. Acquired in 1979

Bastien-Lepage was a pupil of Cabanel at the Ecole des Beaux-Arts; having narrowly missed the Prix de Rome, he decided to record the life of the peasant farmers in his native village, Damvillers in the Lorraine. His huge painting *Les Foins* was the first fruit of this decision : it was exhibited at the 1878 Salon and made a great impression on the public with its unmistakable feeling of open air and open spaces. Bastien-Lepage quickly became a leader of the naturalist school in the 1880s, and his name is sometimes associated with that of Manet, because of his rapid treatment and clear colours. His manner was more readily adopted by foreign artists staying in Paris, than by his French compatriots : this led to its spread throughout Europe and America.

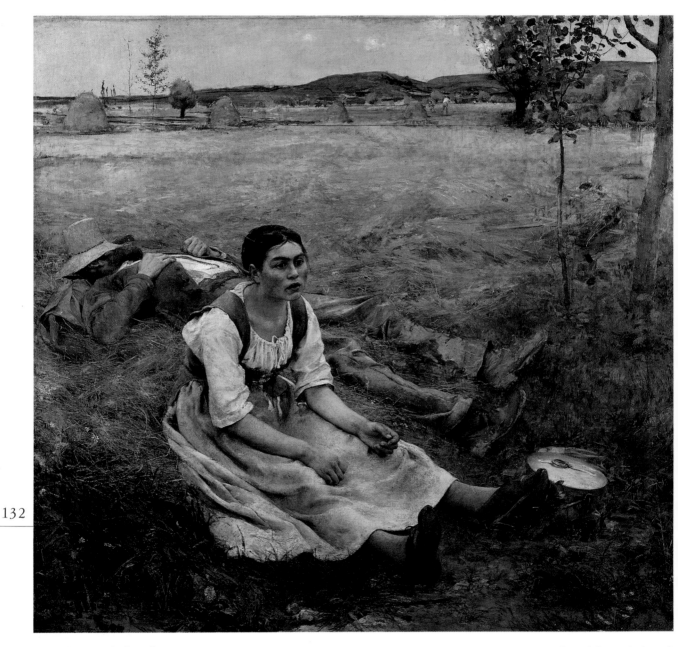

Jules Bastien-Lepage (1848-1884)
Les Foins, 1877. 1878 Salon
180 × 195
Acquired in 1885

Fernand Cormon (1845-1924)
Une forge. Salon des Artistes français, 1894
70 × 90
Acquired in 1894

Léon Lhermitte (1844-1925)
La Paye des moissonneurs
Salon des Artistes français, 1882
215 × 272
Acquired in 1882

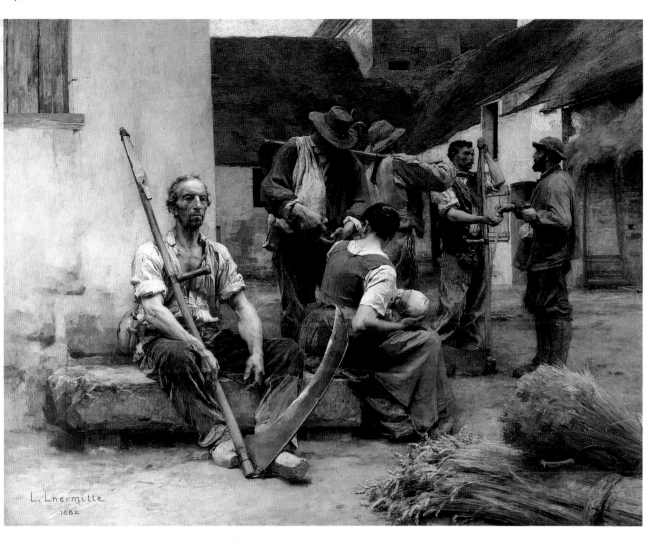

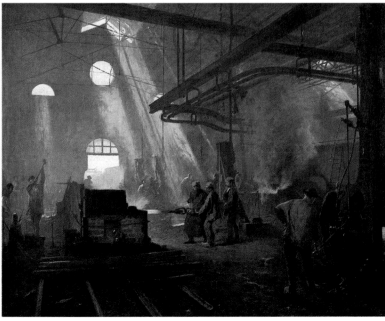

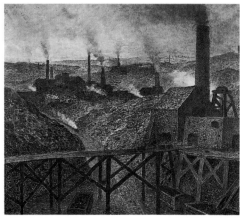

Constantin Meunier (1831-1905)
Au pays noir, 1893
81 × 93
Acquired in 1896

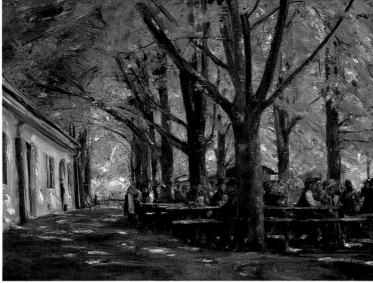

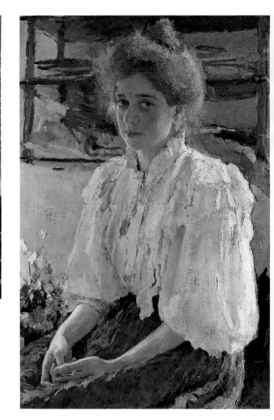

Max Liebermann (1847-1935)
Biergarten at Brannenburg
Société nationale des Beaux-Arts, 1894
70 × 100
Acquired in 1894

George-Hendrik Breitner (1857-1923)
Moonlight, c. 1887-1889
71 × 101
Acquired in 1989

Valentin Alexandrovitch Serov (1865-1911)
Madame Lwoff (1864-1955), 1895
90 × 59
Gift of Pr. André Lwoff and M. Stéphane Lwoff, son of the model, 1980

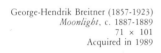

134

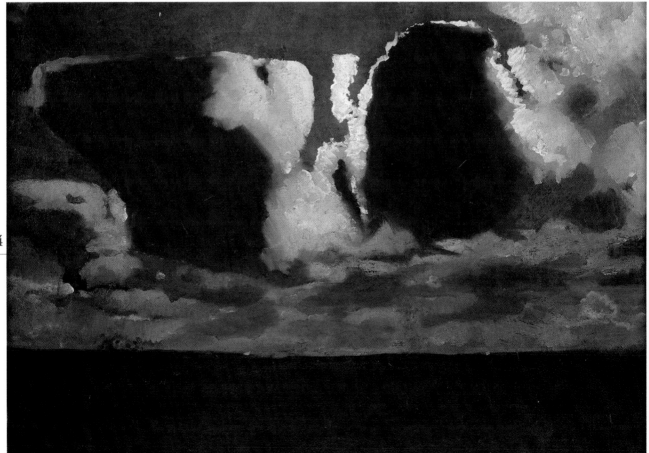

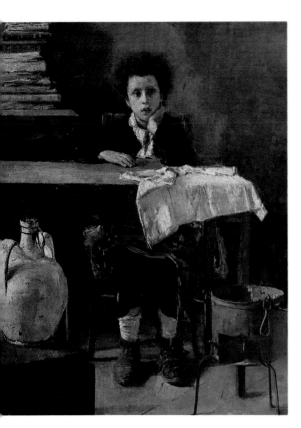

Antonio Mancini (1852-1930)
Pauvre écolier. Salon of 1876
130 × 97
Gift of Charles Landelle, 1906

Winslow Homer (1836-1910)
Nuit d'été, 1890
76,7 × 102
Acquired in 1900

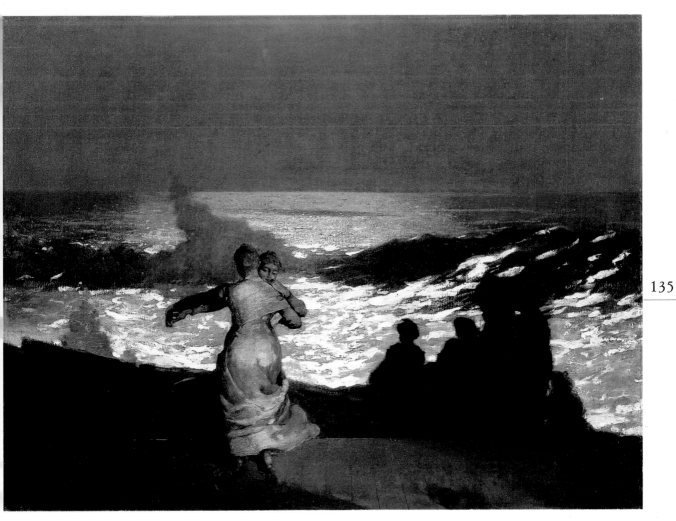

135

Elie Delaunay (1826-1891)
Madame Georges Bizet, Geneviève Halévy
later Mme Emile Straus. 1878 Salon
104 × 75
Bequest of Mme Emile Straus, subject to usufruct
in favour of her husband, 1927
Admitted in 1919

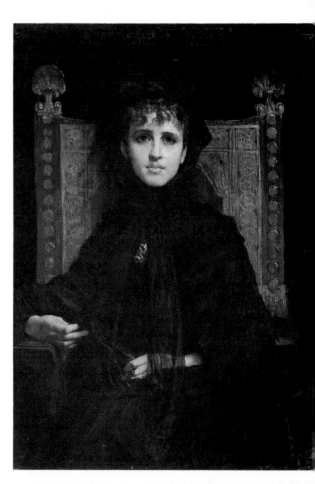

Léon Bonnat (1833-1922)
Madame Pasca, 1874. 1875 Salon
222,5 × 132
Acquired through the bequest of Arthur Pernolet, 1915

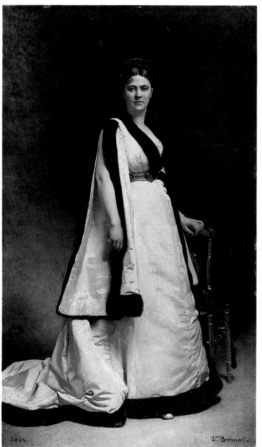

136

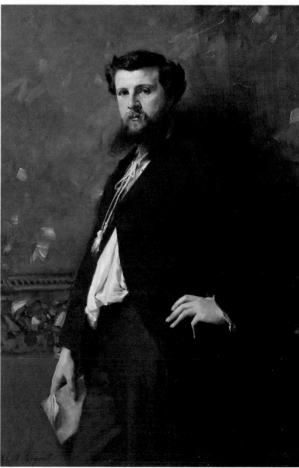

John Singer Sargent (1856-1925)
Édouard Pailleron (1834-1899), 1879
128 × 96
Gift of the Pailleron family to the château de Versailles, 1904
Moved to the musée d'Orsay, 1986

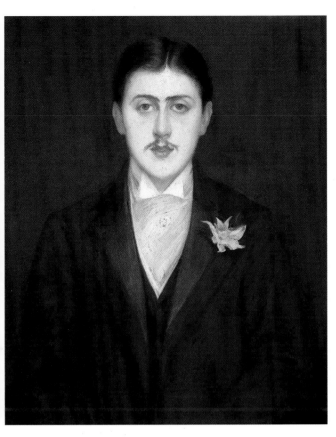

Jacques-Émile Blanche (1861-1942)
Portrait of Marcel Proust, 1892
73,5 × 60,5
Acquired by dation in 1989

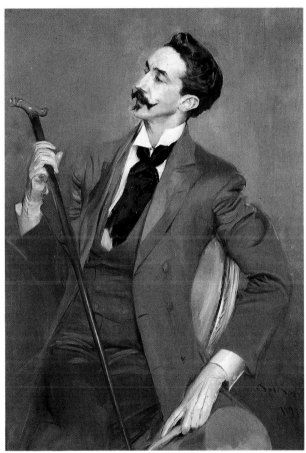

Giovanni Boldini (1842-1931)
Le Comte Robert de Montesquiou (1855-1921), 1897
166 × 82,5
Gift of Henri Pinard, in the name of the comte de Montesquiou, 1922

137

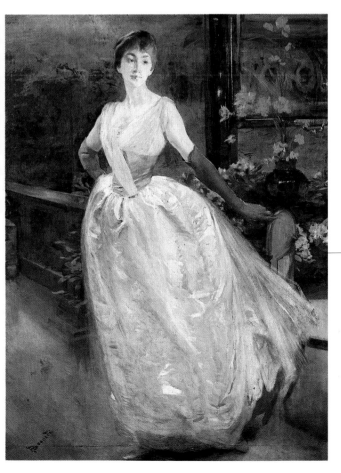

Albert Besnard (1849-1934)
Madame Roger Jourdain, 1885
Salon des Artistes français, 1886
200 × 153
Gift of Mme Roger Jourdain, 1921

138

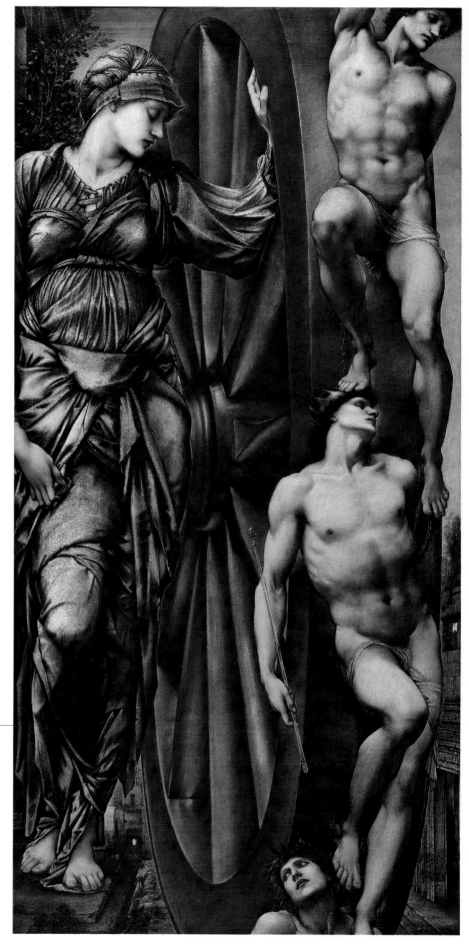

Sir Edward Burne-Jones (1833-1898)
The wheel of Fortune, 1877-1883
200 × 100
Acquired in 1980

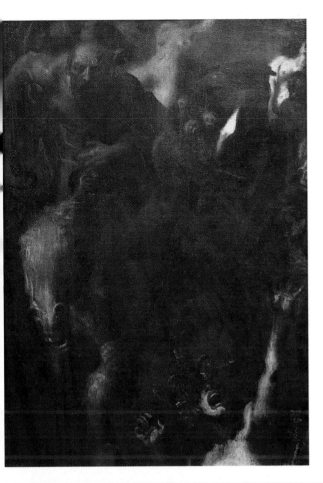

This version of Burne-Jones's *The Wheel of Fortune* is the largest and the most accomplished of his variations on this theme. It appeared for the first time in 1870 in a project for a triptych on the fall of Troy which the artist never completed. The plastic references to Michelangelo in the figures of the king and the slave, and the incisive manner with overtones of Mantegna or Crivelli show the imprint of High Renaissance art on Burne-Jones, who had studied it at Florence and Rome, as well as in London's National Gallery.

Franz von Stuck (1863-1928)
La Chasse sauvage, 1899
97 × 67
Acquired in 1980

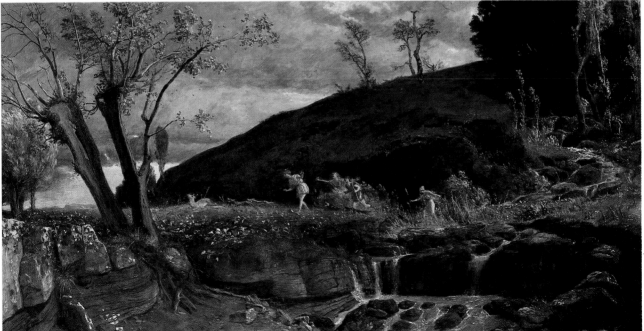

139

Arnold Böcklin (1827-1901)
La Chasse de Diane, 1896
100 × 200
Acquired in 1977

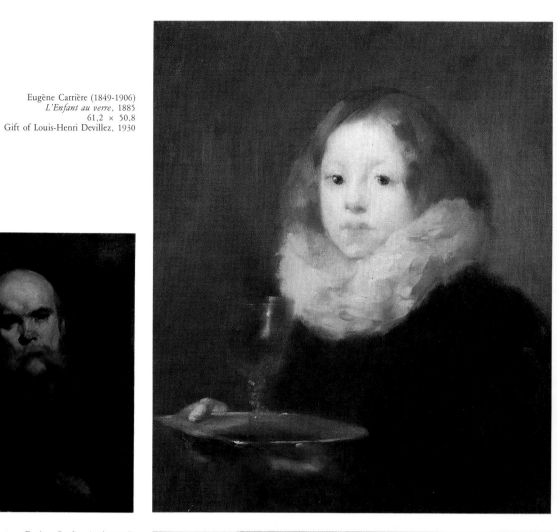

Eugène Carrière (1849-1906)
L'Enfant au verre, 1885
61,2 × 50,8
Gift of Louis-Henri Devillez, 1930

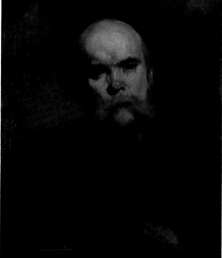

Eugène Carrière (1849-1906)
Paul Verlaine (1844-1896), 1890
Salon de la Société nationale des Beaux-Arts, 1891
61 × 51
Acquired with the participation of the
Société des Amis du Luxembourg, 1910

140

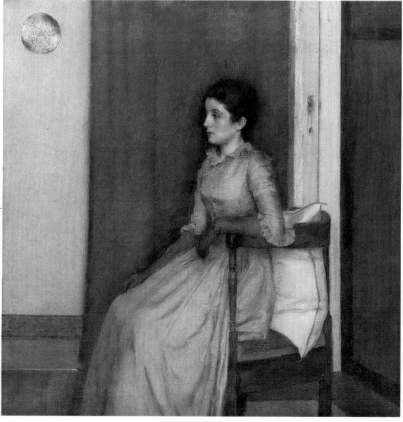

Fernand Knopff (1858-1921)
Marie Monnom, daughter of the Brussels editor
later Mme Théo Van Rysselberghe, 1887
49,5 × 50
Acquired in 1981

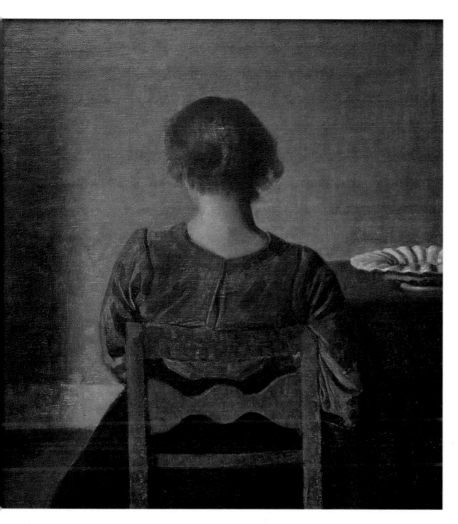

Vilhelm Hammershøi (1864-1916)
Hvile (Repose), 1905
49,5 x 46,5
Acquired with the participation
of the Fondation Philippe Meyer in 1996

Lucien Lévy-Dhurmer (1865-1953)
La Femme à la médaille or *Mystère*, 1896
Pastel, 35 × 54
Gift of M. et Mme Zagorowsky, 1972

141

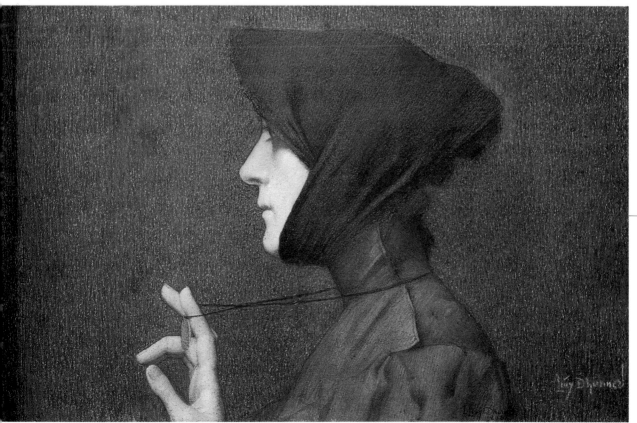

Giuseppe Pelizza da Volpedo
(1868-1907)
Fleur brisée, 1896-1902
79,5 × 107
Acquired in 1910

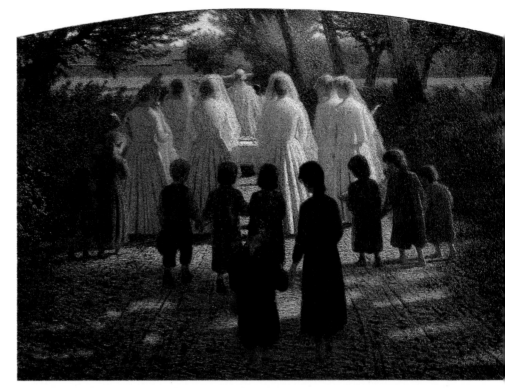

Angelo Morbelli (1853-1919)
*Jour de fête à l'hospice Trivulzio
à Milan*, 1892
78 × 122
Acquired in 1900

142

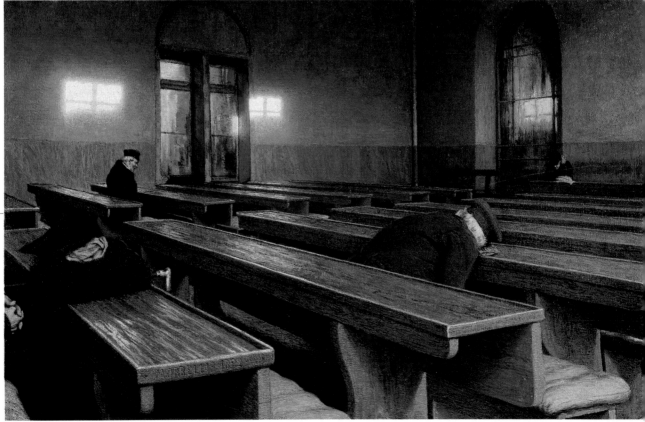

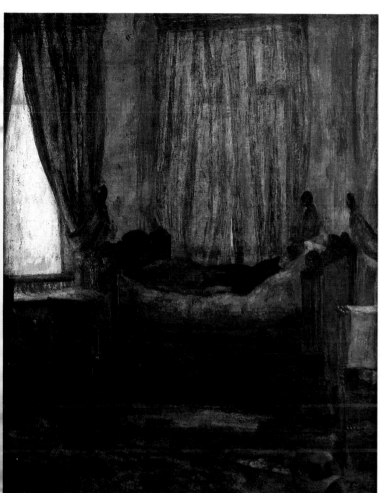

James Ensor (1860-1949)
La Dame en détresse, 1882
100 × 80
Lheureux donation, 1932

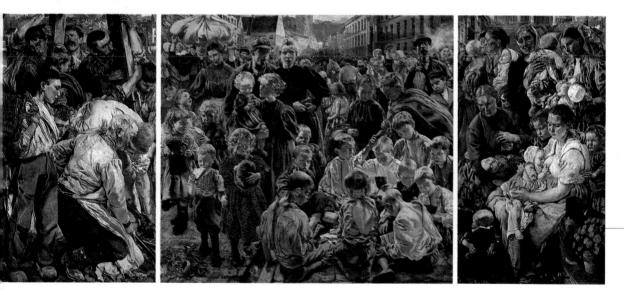

143

Léon Frédéric (1856-1940)
Les Ages de l'ouvrier, triptych, 1895-1897
Salon de la Société nationale des Beaux-Arts, 1898
163 × 187 (central panel)
163 × 94 (side panels)
Acquired in 1898

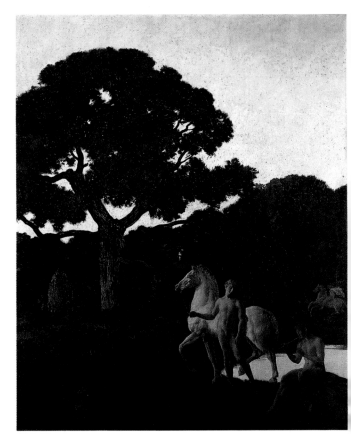

Charles Cottet, having trained at the Julian academy then under Alfred Roll, heeded the advice of Puvis de Chavannes, but preferred a more sombre approach, austere and solid, which was reminiscent of Courbet. One of his first notable works, *Rayons du soir*, painted when he was 29 years old, was acquired by the State at the Salon of 1893. This tranquil scene painted at dusk, where the human figure is reduced to a few silhouttes, evokes the raw solitude of Breton fishermen from the Camaret region — a region which he discovered in 1886 and to which he returned regularly, as did his friends of the "Black Band".

144

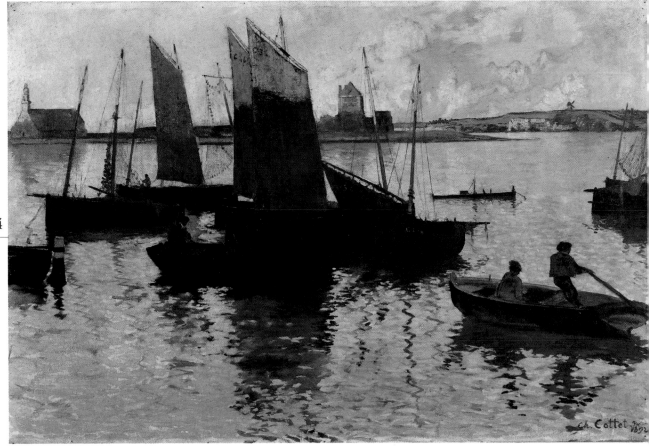

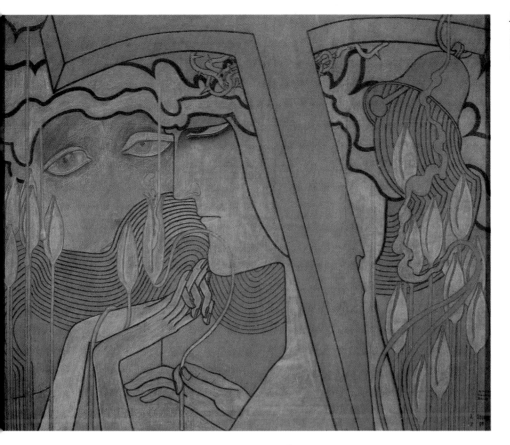

Jan Toorop (1858-1928)
Le Désir et l'assouvissement or
l'Apaisement, 1893
76 × 90
Acquired in 1973

Piet Mondrian (1872-1944)
Le Départ pour la pêche, c. 1898-1900
62 × 100
Acquired in 1987

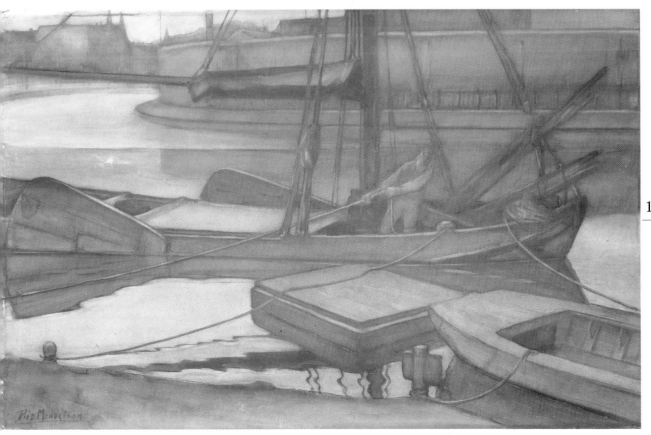

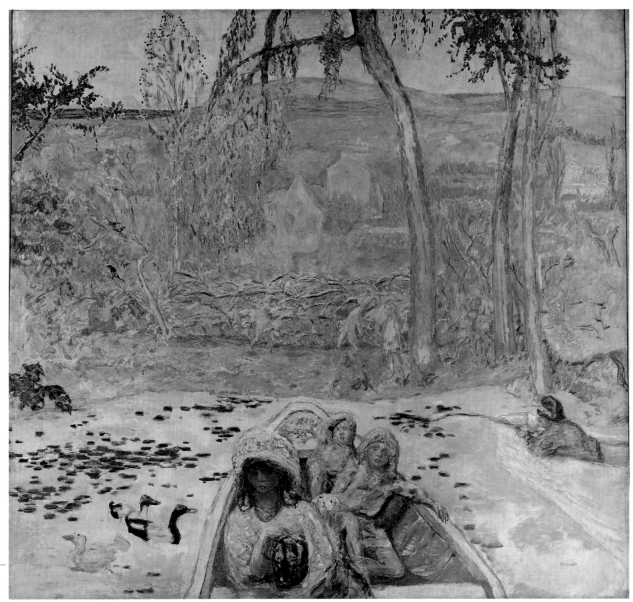

Pierre Bonnard (1867-1947)
En barque, circa 1907
278 × 301
Acquired in 1945

After 1900

At the turn of the century, the nabi movement began to lose cohesion, having in many ways foreshadowed the decorative exuberance of Art Nouveau. While we cannot really call this a rupture, since nabi was never more than a loose brotherhood of painters held together by friendship, nonetheless from 1900 onwards those painters increasingly went their own ways; in doing so, they were fortified by over a decade of shared experience and endorsed by various group exhibitions in galleries (such as Le Barc de Boutteville), on the premises of the *Revue Blanche*, or at the house of the great dealer Siegfried Bing. The last nabi exhibitions as such were held in 1900 and 1902 at the Galerie Bernheim-jeune; after that, Vuillard and Bonnard continued to exhibit there, but in an individual capacity. Vallotton turned to his country of origin, Switzerland, where he produced realistic, daringly-coloured paintings with a pronounced taste (acquired during the artist's nabi years) for disconcerting perspectives and arrangements. Also around 1900, Maillol, who for a time had flirted with the nabis, finally abandoned painting to devote himself to sculpture in which he sought a new classicism in the shapes of his powerfully-built female nudes.

Bonnard, Vuillard, Maurice Denis and Roussel went on to pursue brilliant individual careers, and despite their stylistic differences we find them sharing the common ground of large scale decorative painting and intimist scenes. From their nabi years, all four retained a taste for large decorated surfaces and the Musée d'Orsay is fortunate to possess several important works by Denis, Vuillard and Roussel. In particular, eight paintings completed by Denis between 1898 and 1900 for the chapel of the collège Sainte-Croix at Le Vesinet have been transferred to Orsay from the Musée des Arts décoratifs; these enable us to appreciate the religious inspiration of this profoundly christian artist. After the deconsecration of the chapel after 1905 because of the new laws affecting religious gatherings, the ensemble (which was remounted on canvas) was placed in reserve and successfully restored later.

Vuillard, on the other hand, was more interested by interior decoration. After completing a series of panels for the writer Claude Anet in 1902, he went on to execute another sequence for Henry Bernstein in 1908 which is rather more realistically treated than were his first nabi ensembles. In 1911, he painted *La Bibliothèque* for the office of the princess de Bassiano; here, a large-scale format is used to project an intimate, balanced and wonderfully harmonious scene (crowned by a frieze) in which a classical tapestry serves as a backdrop. Two years later, Vuillard was commissioned to decorate Bois Lurette, the Bernheim-jeune villa at Villers-sur-Mer, with a series of panels; the Musée d'Orsay possesses one of these, *Femmes sous la véranda*, thanks to the generosity of the descendants of the Bernheim-jeune family.

Ker-Xavier Roussel looked to mythology for subject matter when he painted his highly animated and coloured larger compositions, *L'Enlèvement des filles de Leucippe*, and *Polyphème, Acis et Galatée*. The latter was a very large panel commissioned by the theatre director Luthé-Poë, with whom the nabis had collaborated from the very beginning. In 1913, the art patron

Gabriel Thomas organised three former nabis to decorate the new Théâtre des Champs-Élysées then under construction by the Perret brothers. The dome was entrusted to Maurice Denis; he covered it with classical themes evoking music and opera, in the bland colours which he was to use thereafter for all his larger decorative works. The Musée d'Orsay possesses the reduced maquette of this dome, miraculously preserved because it had remained in the Thomas family's house at Meudon until 1983. The bas-reliefs of the theatre were done by the sculptor Bourdelle, Vuillard decorated the foyer, and Roussel covered the curtain with a bacchanalian scene contiguous to another at the nearby Comédie des Champs-Élysées.

Bonnard continued in his own way, remaining the most deliberately innovative of the ex-nabis and frequently anticipating the pictural audacities of the later 20th century. While voluntarily holding aloof from the various great trends of fauvism, cubism and abstract art, Bonnard, who had never been a theorist, became completely involved in his investigation of colour and the spatial possibilities of painting. Thus most of his work after 1905 has come to the Musée national d'Art moderne, at the Centre Georges-Pompidou, although the musée d'Orsay can still exhibit some canvases, notably *En barque*, which show Bonnard's contribution to the crucial first years of the 20th century.

It is easy to discern the parting of ways between Vuillard and Bonnard in the field of portraiture, which remained a predilection for the former nabis. Vuillard's portraits are warmly intimist in flavour, and treated with a new respect for classical perspectives along with his habitual sensitivity to atmosphere. This is particularly evident in *la Chapelle de Versailles* and in the important series of portraits by Vuillard at Orsay, such as those of the writer *Romain Coolus*, *La Princesse de Polignac* and *Mme Bénard*. Bonnard's technique is completely different, while remaining consistent with his nabi innovations. *La Femme au chat* (1912), and the extraordinary *Portrait des frères Bernheim* (1920) show his exploration of visual fields and his attempt to render their totality by the use of new effects in perspective. Bonnard's *Nature morte, assiette de pommes*, from the former Gould collection, was recently acquired for the Musée d'Orsay by dation and gives evidence of spatial experiments similar to those of *La Femme au chat*. The two paintings are of roughly the same date; they show clearly that colour itself is becoming the dominant theme of Bonnard's work, and it is this that makes the *Portrait des frères Bernheim* so extraordinary.

Both in France and abroad, the 20th century began in a ferment of new artistic movements, mostly dominated by research into the nature of colour. 1904 and 1905 emerge as key years just prior to the explosion of fauvism, foreshadowed by Van Gogh, Gauguin and the impressionists. The autonomy of colour and its relationship with form is the central concern of a painting by Matisse, *Luxe, calme et volupté* (1904), which the Musée d'Orsay recently acquired by dation. This painting, with its impressionist roots, preceded *Le Luxe I* which in turn paved the way for Matisse's great *La Musique* and *La Danse* commissioned in 1909 by the Russian collector Stschoukine (Saint Petersburg, Hermitage Museum). Around *Luxe, calme et volupté* are grouped several fauvist paintings from the Centre Pompidou, such as Marquet's portrait of the critic *André Rouveyre*, Dufy's *Rue du village*, Derain's *Pont de Charing Cross* and Vlaminck's *Restaurant à Marly-le-Roi* and *Still life* (the latter three works were part of the Kaganovitch donation). This ensemble effectively demonstrates the liberation of the expressive power of colour in the first decade of the 20th century.

The Musée d'Orsay's recent acquisition policies have been aimed at filling important lacunae in the collection of foreign painters, many of whom belonged to movements that broke away from the symbolism and naturalism of the 19th century at the very beginning of the 20th. This was notably the case of the Viennese secessionists, who blossomed in 1898 under the banner of decorative art. The painters Gustav Klimt and Koloman Moser were among the founders of this movement, which is now recognised as a major influence in the formation of a new concept of "modernity", along with the architectural work of Otto Wagner and Hoffman. Functionalism, when it emerged, served both to summarise the atmosphere at the turn of the century (as in Klimt's sensitive work) and to confirm the new orientation of modern architecture and decorative art, along the lines laid down by the artists of the Glasgow school.

Lastly, the 1986 acquisition of an impressive pre-fauvist landscape by the Norwegian painter Edvard Munch is an important event for the Musée d'Orsay, in view of the rarity of this artist's work on the international market. Indeed, there is only one other painting by this great expressionist in the national collection of France (Musée Rodin). In this way, the directors of the Musée d'Orsay are seeking to re-establish a proper equilibrium between the avant-garde French movements and those which developed concurrently abroad, leading to the same conclusions of expressionism and abstract art.

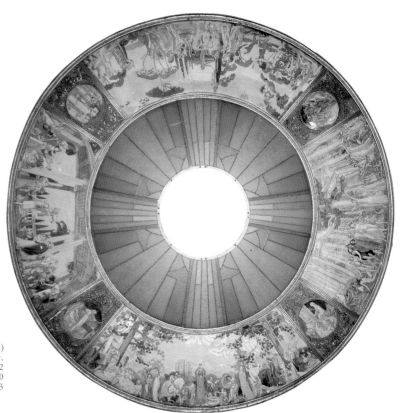

Maurice Denis (1870-1943)
Design for the dome of the Champs-Elysées Theatre,
c. 1911-1912
Diam. 240
Acquired in 1983

150

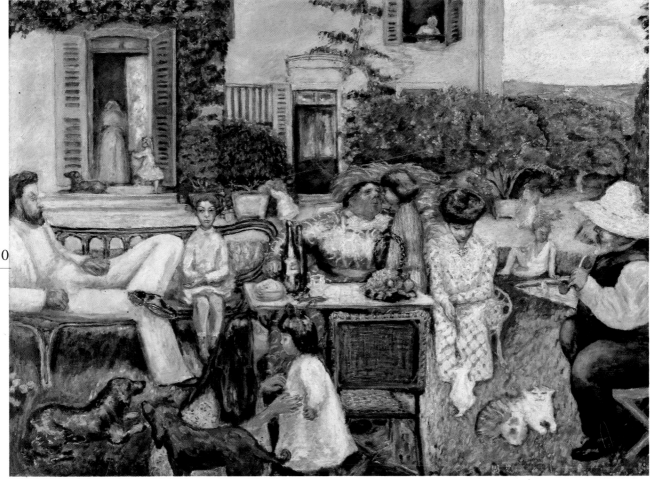

D ecorations intended for public buildings, like the paintings of Maurice Denis, Vuillard and Roussel for the new Champs-Elysées Theatre, or decorations as a result of private commissions, like *La Bibliothèque* by Vuillard — all works of vast dimensions — reveal a clear return to classical ideals. This piece by Roussel stands out among his œuvre for its deeply sensual mythological inspiration, whilst Maurice Denis experiments with ample rythmns — cultivated equally by Vuillard and Bonnard — in a more intimate register or in a tender humourous mode.

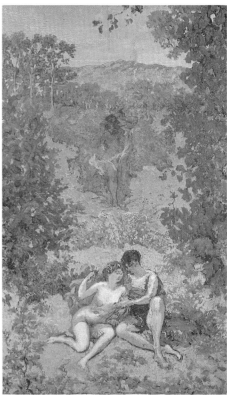

Ker-Xavier Roussel (1867-1944)
Polyphème, Acis et Galatée
Paper on canvas, 273 × 165
Admitted in 1943

151

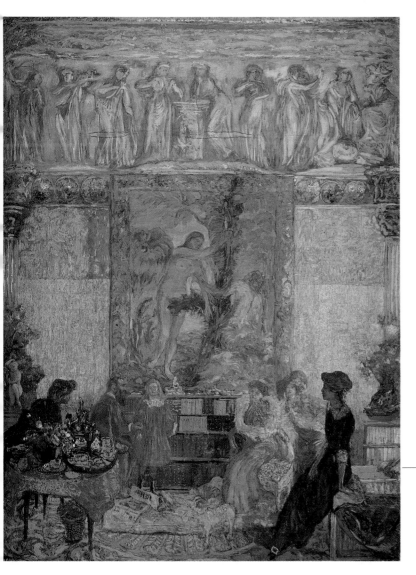

Édouard Vuillard (1868-1940)
La Bibliothèque
Décor for princess Bassiano, 1911
400 × 300
Acquired in 1935

Pierre Bonnard (1867-1947)
L'Après-midi bourgeoise, 1900
139 × 212
Acquired by dation in 1988

Édouard Vuillard (1868-1940)
La Chapelle du château de Versailles, 1917-1919
recovered in 1928
Paper on canvas, 96 × 66
Donation by Jacques Laroche (usufruct reserved), 1947
Admitted in 1976

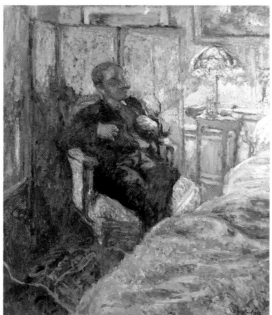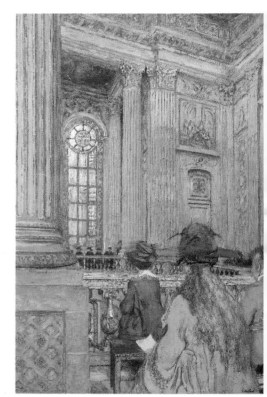

Édouard Vuillard (1868-1940)
Romain Coolus,
writer in *La Revue Blanche*
Hardboard, 74 × 68
Loan and subsequent gift
of the model to
the Musée du Luxembourg, 1930

152

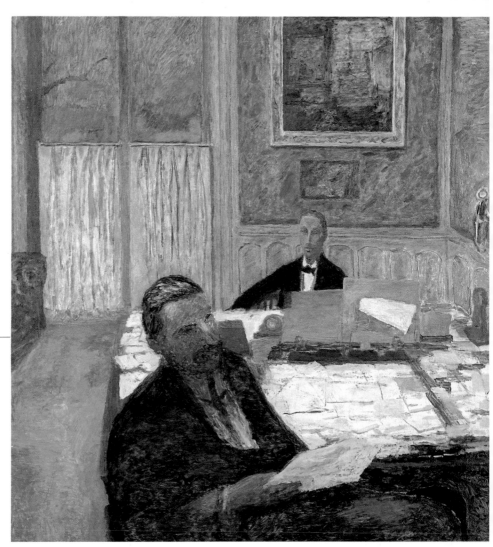

Pierre Bonnard (1867-1947)
*Josse Bernheim-jeune
and Gaston Bernheim de Villiers*, 1920
165 × 155
Gift of Bernheim de Villiers, 1951

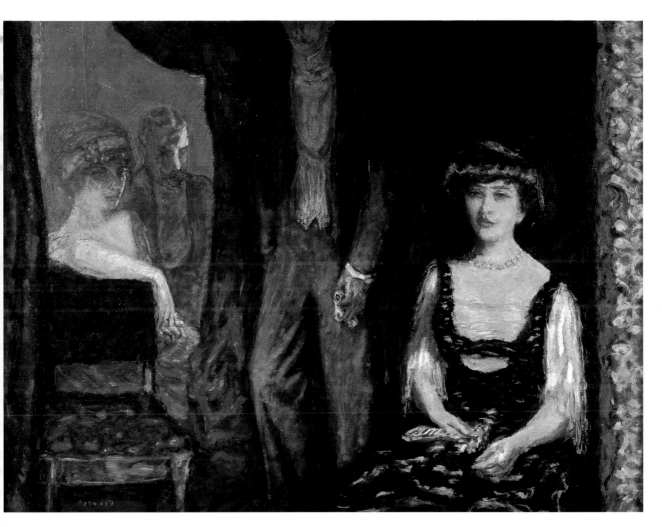

Pierre Bonnard (1867-1947)
La Loge, 1908
91 × 120
Acquired by dation in 1989

153

A subject particularly evocative of Parisian life, the theme of the theatre box is revived here by Bonnard, following Renoir and Mary Cassatt, in this portrait of the Berheim-Jeune brothers and their wives. The unusual centring of the image, the impression of polite boredom which separates the spectators engaged in a social ritual, shows how brilliantly Bonnard manages to create a piece of pure painting from a commissioned work, infusing it with subtle humour.

atisse painted *Luxe, calme et volupté* while staying with his friend Signac at Saint-Tropez in 1904 and it clearly shows his shift from neo-impressionism to fauvism. This canvas may be said to mark the precise moment when the theoretical research of divisionism gave way to the power of pure colour, notably in terms of Matisse's own struggle to choose between "linear plasticity" and "colour plasticity". First Derain, then Marquet and Braque joined the movement which was to culminate in the celebrated scandal of the Salon d'automne in 1905.

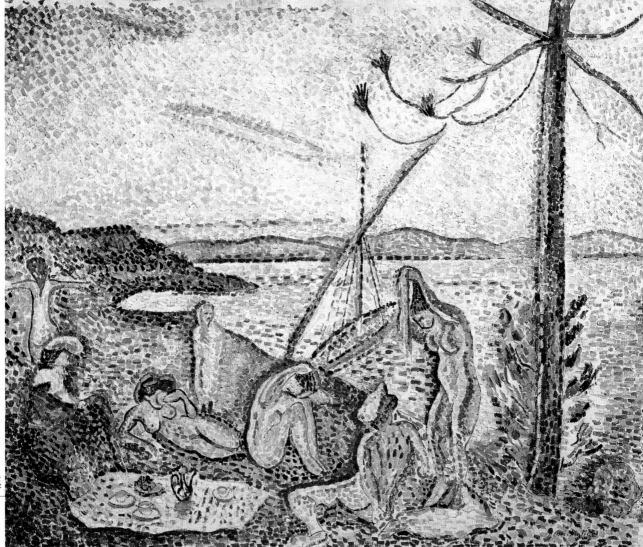

154

Henri Matisse (1869-1954)
Luxe, calme et volupté, 1904
98,5 × 118
Acquired by dation in 1982
transferred from the Musée national d'Art moderne

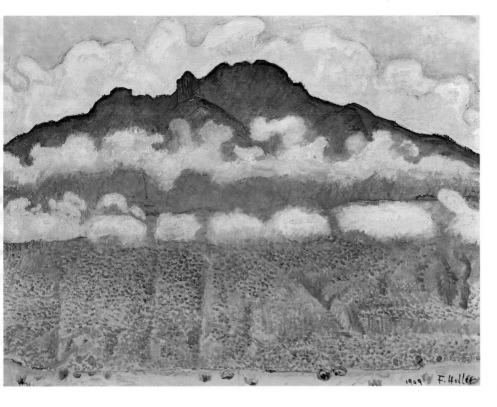

Ferdinand Hodler (1853-1918)
Schynige Platte, 1909
67,5 × 90,5
Acquired in 1987

André Derain (1880-1954)
Pont de Charing Cross, 1906
81 × 100
Max and Rosy Kaganovitch donation, 1973

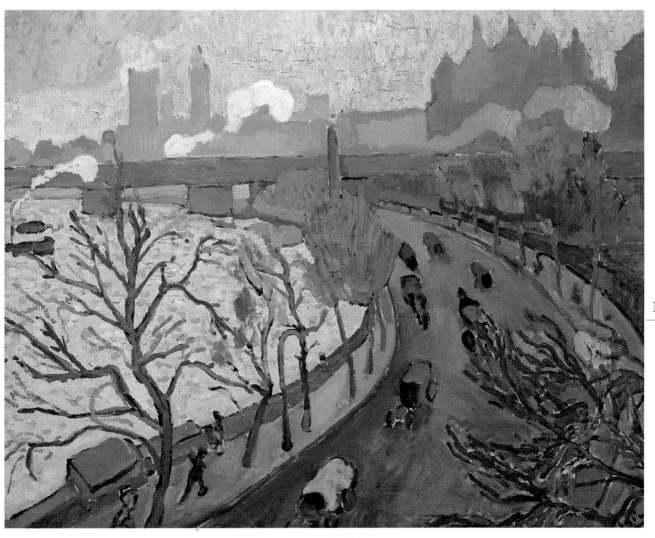

155

es *Rosiers sous les arbres* was one of ten landscapes painted by Klimt between 1905 and 1910, marking the apogee of the Viennese secession movement. Koloman Moser's hardboard study for a window panel in the Steinhof church, Vienna, itself one of Otto Wagner's major projects, offers a rational view of the same decorative trend; here the emphasis is on geometrical, compartmentalised forms, and their subordination to monumental architectural space.

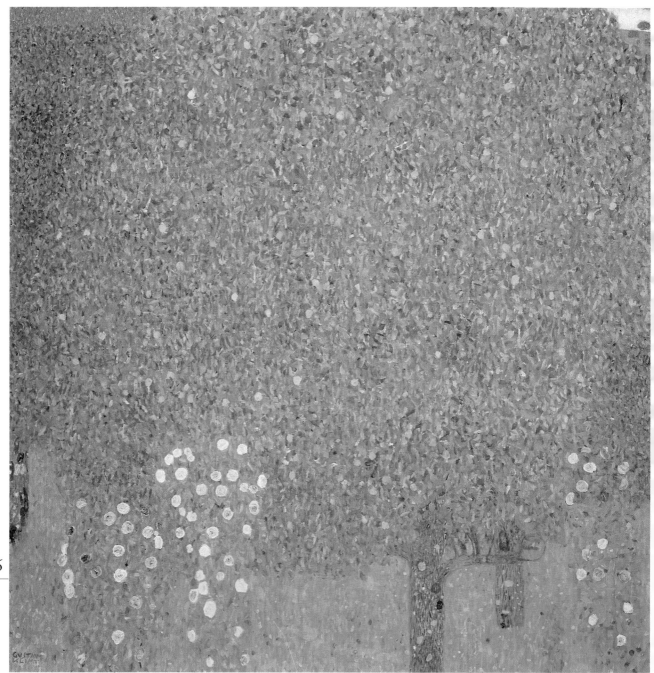

Gustav Klimt (1862-1918)
Rosiers sous les arbres, circa 1905
110 × 110
Acquired in 1980

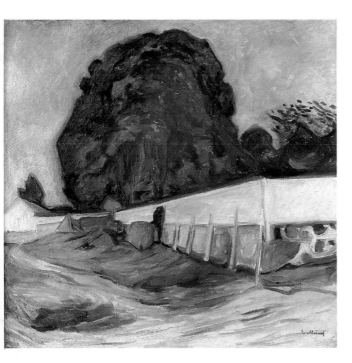

Edvard Munch (1863-1944)
Summer night at Aasgaardstrand, 1904
99 x 103
Acquired in 1986

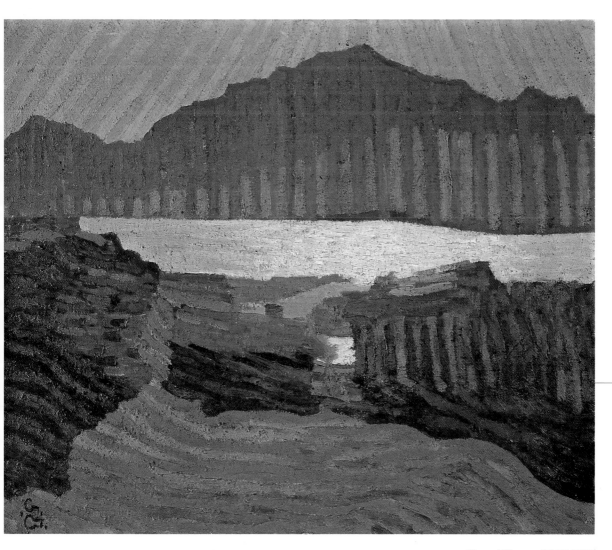

157

Giovanni Giacometti (1868-1933)
View of Capolago (Ticino), c. 1907
51,5 x 60
Acquired thanks to the Fondation Philippe Meyer in 1997

INDEX

References in roman are to pages where the artists are cited, italic references are to illustrations.

159

Contents

Imprimé en France
par l'Imprimerie Kapp Lahure Jombart à Évreux, mars 1999
Photogravure Scala - Italie
Dépôt légal : avril 1998